H. D. LEWIS has been Professor of the History and Philosophy of Religion in the University of London since 1955. Born in 1910, he was educated at University College, Bangor, and Jesus College, Oxford, before returning to Bangor as Lecturer in Philosophy in 1936; he became Senior Lecturer in 1947 and was Professor of Philosophy from 1947 until 1955. He has lectured extensively in the United States, Canada and Great Britain at universities which include Pennsylvania (Visiting Professor, 1958–9), Oxford (Wilde Lecturer in natural and comparative religion, 1960–63), Harvard (1963), Yale (Visiting Professor, 1964–5), Edinburgh (Gifford Lecturer, 1966–8), and London (L. T. Hobhouse Memorial Lecturer, 1966–8). A Fellow of King's College, London, since 1963, he was Dean of the faculty of theology in the University of London from 1964 to 1968 and Dean of the faculty of arts at King's College from 1966 to 1968. He has been President of many learned societies and is Chairman of the Council of the Royal Institute of Philosophy. The editor of The Muirhead Library of Philosophy and of the journal *Religious Studies*, Professor Lewis is also the author of *Morals and the New Theology* (1947), *Morals and Revelation* (1951), *Our Experience of God* (1959), *Freedom and History* (1962), and *Teach Yourself the Philosophy of Religion* (1965).

ROBERT LAWSON SLATER is Professor Emeritus of World Religions at Harvard University. He was previously Director of the Centre for the Study of World Religions at Harvard, which was initiated with the aim of bringing together, from East and West, students belonging to different religious traditions engaged in the study of religions. He is a graduate of Cambridge University, England, and received his doctoral degree in the history of religions from Columbia University, New York, following some seventeen years of travel and residence in Asia from the time of his first academic appointment as Lecturer in Logic at Rangoon University, Burma. He has been Visiting Professor at Banaras Hindu University, India, and other institutions in Asia and Africa. Prior to his Harvard appointments he was Professor of Systematic Theology at McGill University, Canada, and Principal of the Montreal Diocesan Theological College. Canon Slater's publications include *World Religions and World Community*, *Can Christians Learn from Other Religions?*, and *Paradox and Nirvana: A Study of Religious Ultimates with special reference to Burmese Buddhism*.

H. D. LEWIS AND
ROBERT LAWSON SLATER

The Study of Religions

MEETING POINTS AND
MAJOR ISSUES

PENGUIN BOOKS

Penguin Books Ltd, Harmondsworth, Middlesex, England
Penguin Books Inc., 7110 Ambassador Road, Baltimore, Maryland 21207, U.S.A.
Penguin Books Australia Ltd, Ringwood, Victoria, Australia

—

First published (as *World Religions*) by Watts 1966
Published in Pelican Books 1969
Copyright © H. D. Lewis and Robert Lawson Slater, 1966

—

Made and printed in Great Britain by
Cox & Wyman Ltd, London, Reading and Fakenham
Set in Monotype Garamond

Contents

Preface

THIS book attempts to give some indication of the
problems which present themselves in the study of religion
today, taking heed especially of new ways of thinking about
religion and of some of the findings of recent historical
investigation. Distinctive features of major religions are
noted, but mainly for the light they throw on the way we
should be thinking about these religions at present. The
state of the subject today is described by Professor Slater
who also passes some of the great religions of the world in
review in amplification of what he says about the study of
religions in Chapter I. The treatment is exploratory rather
than exhaustive and it is hoped that the reader will find it a
useful guide when he sets out to amplify his knowledge of
the subject from the many manuals and admirable outlines
of the great religions available now – and from the study of
original texts. Part One of the book is the work of Professor
Slater. In Part Two Professor Lewis offers, in the form of
a continuous essay divided into sections, a more specific
indication of the bearing of philosophy on the study of
religions today and especially on points of affinity and
differences in the religions of the East and the West. This
contains the substance of the Owen Evans Lectures given
recently at University College, Aberystwyth, and Professor Lewis wishes to express here his gratitude to the
College for the honour they did him and for much encouragement and hospitality. The two authors have spent
much time together in discussion of their work and of other
related matters. They do not pretend to be in strict agreement on all points and Professor Slater would not endorse
what Professor Lewis says at the close about the work of
Paul Tillich. But where there are differences of this sort the

reader may find in them refreshing and stimulating indications of those changes and complications in the study of religion today of which Professor Slater gives an account in the introductory chapter of the book. If readers are encouraged, not only to learn about religious practices and traditions but also to try afresh to understand them with patience and care, the authors will feel amply rewarded for their work.

Professor Lewis wishes to express his gratitude to the editors of the *Monist* and *Aryan Path* for permission to reproduce material which had already appeared in his contributions to these journals.

The authors also feel very much indebted to the Rev. W. R. Weeks for his kindness in preparing the index for this volume.

PART ONE

I

Modern Studies of Religion

THOSE who belong to what is called the Western Judaic Christian tradition number rather more than 850 million. They share the world with about half that number of Muslims, a similar number of Hindus, and several hundred million Buddhists, some of whom mix Confucian and other teachings with their Buddhism. In addition, there are fifty million Taoists, over thirty million Japanese adherents of Shinto forms of religion, eight million Sikhs, perhaps two million Zoroastrians, not to mention the numerous tribes whose religion is described as primitive. The statistics in regard to religion are seldom reliable but these estimates suffice to indicate the variety of belief and practice which confronts the student of religion today.[1] Account must also be taken of an increasing number, frequently named secularists, who, the world over, have rejected ancestral faiths and perhaps find it easier to say what they do not believe than what they do believe. Further note may be taken of the quasi religions, such as Communism and Fascism and the innumerable hybrid forms, for it is not only Buddhists who mix their beliefs. What is more, there is the fact that such umbrella terms as Christianity and Buddhism are deceptive. They tend to obscure the rich diversity of

1. One of the most recent attempts to arrive at accurate statistics is that made by the Reverend Edward Kupsch, who presented the following statistics for 1962 at a Lutheran Conference held in Westphalia: Chinese religion, 337 million; Islam, 350 million; Hindus, 325 million; Buddhists, 150 million; Taoists, 50 million; Shintoists, 34 million; primitive religions, 130 million; *fragliche* (quasi or questionable) religions, 543 million.

belief and practice to be found *within* these and other traditions. To study religion, then, means to be confronted by a bewildering variety.

Add to all this the fact that there is apparently no limit to the questions which may be asked about religion any more than there is any limit to the standpoints from which the subject may be viewed, and it might very well seem that any attempt at an orderly treatment of such a subject is doomed to failure from the outset. There is clearly a risk of imposing an order of one's own which may ignore or blanket the complexity of the subject.

What is described as the modern 'science of religion', however, began in the West with a resolute attempt to reduce the subject to order (as the name science implies) combined with an equally resolute attempt to deal with all the facts and nothing but the facts (as, again, the name science implies).

And thereby hangs a tale. It is a tale which begins close upon a hundred years ago when the western world began to be aroused from a religious isolation which had lasted for centuries. It was an isolation which produced Parson Thwackums saying, as late as the eighteenth century, that by religion they meant Christianity and by Christianity they meant the Protestant religion, and by the Protestant religion they meant the Church of England. For the greater period of western history the majority of other believers were at a far distance. They were at the other side of the world and little or nothing was known about their Hinduism or their Buddhism. There was indeed at one time an alarming awareness of the Muslim believers who threatened the very existence of western Christendom, coming as far as Spain, but there was little or no knowledge of their *religion*.[1] Dispersed throughout Europe, there were also the Jews, but

1. Interest in Muslim culture did not amount to interest in Muslim *religion*.

here again little was known of what they believed; Jews were generally regarded as strange people who, like Christians, began with the Old Testament, but unlike Christians obstinately refused to go further.

Scholars, it is true, could look back to a time when conditions were different. They knew that Christianity, cradled in Jewry, had been affected by early encounter with the rival faiths of the ancient world and still bore the impress of Greek religious speculations. There were also writers such as Lord Herbert of Cherbury who were prepared to find truth in all religions and much the same truth. But, by and large, the western religious outlook went no further than the dominant Christian tradition. Any discussion of the meaning and credibility of religious beliefs was against this background.

A change came with the exciting pace of discovery in the nineteenth century. Trade and travel between East and West, together with the Christian missionary enterprise, brought increasing knowledge, first of the religious life and thought of India and next of the Far East. One by one, the scriptures of other religions were translated into European languages and made available to western readers. Philosophers and others studied this newly discovered wisdom of the East with growing interest. Some of them made swift and free use of it to advance their own speculations. Christian theologians, for the most part, conceived it as a new challenge calling for a new defence of their faith.

In 1875 Friedrich Max Müller published the first of the fifty volumes which were to constitute the great informative series of the *Sacred Books of the East*. From now on, western knowledge of oriental religions grew apace.

But Max Müller did something more than provide new information. Along with others such as Emile Burnouf, he advocated an entirely new approach to the study of religion. It was the age of science, with new methods of inquiry. Religion should be studied accordingly. A factual, objective and orderly approach similar to that pursued in other sciences held rich promise of similar rewards. Max Müller himself had more particularly in view the model of the science of languages with its orderly grouping of kindred languages. He anticipated the same wide range of inquiry, the same possibility of comparison and the same kind of classification in the study of religions.

In proposing this new approach, Max Müller distinguished sharply between two kinds of inquiry, a factual, scientific inquiry, having to do with the when and where of religious beliefs, and a theological or philosophical inquiry having to do with the significance and credibility of such beliefs. Henceforth there were to be two separate disciplines, the new comparative study of religion or general History of Religion and the Philosophy of Religion. Each discipline was conceived to have its own and different approach. What would be attempted in the one would be avoided in the other.

Thus the modern study of religion began with the building of a fence, with historians and scientists on the one side of the fence, and theologians and philosophers on the other side. Philosophers and theologians could indeed pass through the fence if they wished to do so and join the scientists, but only on condition that they forgot for the time being that they were theologians and philosophers and observed the rules of the new game. The fence was built in the interests of the objectivity which was regarded as essential to science. It was an objectivity which could only be achieved by students who approached the subject with an open mind. While the advocates of the new science were not naïve enough to suppose that an open mind meant an entirely empty mind, they were wary of minds filled with preconceived ideas or *a priori* notions. Such minds, it was held, were biased from the start, all too ready to pronounce premature verdicts and draw premature conclusions in the light of their own prior beliefs and opinions. Theologians were particularly suspect. In the past, if they had made any study at all of what other believers had to say, it was generally with the avowed purpose of refuting such a say and maintaining the Christian truth as they conceived it. But philosophers came a close second. They could be just as much wedded to their own dogmas and speculations as any theologian.

Professor Goblet d'Alviella, who was one of the first to hold a university chair in the History of Religions, was so persuaded about the need for a really open mind that he devoted his inaugural lecture at Brussels to a discussion of the prejudgements which should be avoided. Beginning with religious prejudice, he cited the view that the story of Jonah and the whale must be accepted as literally true because it came in the Bible and was part of 'supernatural revelation'. Goblet went on to pillory philosophic sceptics and philosophic positivists as well as philologists and anthropologists who also have their Jonahs. Any 'doctrine fixed in advance' was inimical to the free inquiry which he advocated. Others spoke similarly. Theologians and philosophers in particular were seen as binding others, as they themselves were bound, to 'doctrines fixed in advance'. The very name, science of religion, spelt freedom from such fixity.

As the new science developed, however, questions arose, first with regard to the possibility of this freedom, second, with regard to its desirability.

Historians of religion might be observed as doing the very thing which they forbade the theologians and philosophers to do, entering the field with presuppositions of their own or presuppositions accepted from others. Even Professor Goblet, despite his warnings against prejudgement, ventured a prejudgement at the end of his lecture when he said that it would make for better understanding of the religions of mankind if it could be accepted that, while none of them possessed absolute truth, each of them contained relative truth, citing the sages of antiquity in support of this opinion.

One very general assumption was the view that the new science would demonstrate what was called the 'essence' of religion. Here Hegel, Feuerbach and others may be seen off stage, prompting the lines. Perhaps, however, little prompting was needed. Max Müller and his friends were deeply persuaded that one of the most valuable results of their science would be the demonstration of what was essential in religion, whatever the philosophers might or might not say about it. They were convinced beforehand that the further their inquiry was pursued the more it would become evident that believers the world over had much the same fundamental beliefs in common. The facts would speak for themselves. Indeed they had begun to do so. Enough was already known of the fundamental beliefs held in other traditions to point the conclusion that men were everywhere repeating in their own terms the same prayer: 'Our Father which art in heaven.' Continued inquiry would produce increasing evidence of other comparable beliefs. A circle could then be drawn around these similar expressions of faith and all outside this circle could be dismissed as non-essential.

Such a conclusion involves something more than straight inference from the evidence. It is not just a case of 'the facts speaking for themselves'. It is a conclusion which is at least partly the result of a leap from the spring-board of a prior conception, namely a conception of 'religion in general' or something which might be called the nature of religion. One effect of this presupposition was the tendency to ignore or discount what was exceptional and particular in the field.

At a later stage the general acceptance of the theory of evolution both quickens the search for essentials and gives it new direction. Since religion has evolved, it is said, the thing to do is to return to the beginning and study primitive forms. The anthropologist here comes into the picture accompanied by the sociologist and the psychologist, and the science of religion becomes a number of sciences, each with its own special interest and standpoint. The general practitioner, however, continues bravely, grateful for the crumbs of new knowledge – sometimes more than crumbs – which come from the tables of the specialists. This multiplication of standpoints, however, complicates things a great deal. It means an end to the earlier view that the essence of religion can be found in a few basic tenets. It also means, or should mean, an end to the notion that the study of religion amounts to no more than a searching of the scriptures and a comparison of religious ideas. The search for the essence of religion is pursued in new directions. Regard for the significance of primitive rituals leads to fuller realization of the many and various expressions of religious life and thought. Nor is it just a question of comparing one religion with another with respect to what may be considered the leading ideas of each tradition, Buddhist, Christian, and so on. There is now a growing appreciation of the rich diversity to be found within each of these traditions. There is also a growing respect for what is particular and exceptional. In short, the full complexity of religious phenomena becomes more and more evident.

Nevertheless the resolution to present religious phenomena in some kind of order continues. Again new directions are taken. Besides the vertical lines suggested by the several traditions set side by side, there are now horizontal lines as types or patterns of religious life and thought are traced across the board, cutting through the lines separating one religion from another. Prophets are found outside Israel;

religious poetry beyond Persia; similar rites of initiation are found to express much the same motifs; Hindu and Buddhist religions of grace besides the Christian are noted. Religious hopes and fears are seen to point to similar goals and the relation between religion and society is seen to raise similar issues in different contexts.

But how are these patterns discerned? Not, it would seem, by observers sitting passively before the facts, waiting for the facts to speak for themselves. The types thus presented are said to be 'constructed' – constructed by the observer.

They have also been described as 'ideal types', conceived beforehand as convenient ways of organizing the material. Clearly, there is something here which involves prejudgement. Even if the types presented are suggested by what is actually observed in some particular instance, they involve the assumption that other examples of the kind will be found. Any scientific statement, it may be argued, is a framed statement, since science means something more than a mere reporting of facts. But the frames or types here presented are very much preconceived frames, dependent on what may be in the mind of the student to start with, as against those accepted by the historian who begins with the frames set before him by particular traditions. It may, however, be replied that the historian has his own preconceptions. More often than not, he comes on the scene disposed to view other traditions in the light of his own tradition, looking for the kind of organization with which he is familiar.

To raise such issues is to raise new questions in regard to any 'pure objectivity' in the comparative study of religion. They are questions which have been brought very much into the open by the development on the Continent of what is called the phenomenology of religion, for here again we have a presentation of types of religious faith and practice, a presentation by scholars who are more interested in contours than boundaries as they roam across the broad field of religious phenomena, assembling, from this or that tradition, examples of similar forms of behaviour and belief. In this case, however, it is claimed that the types presented correspond to 'structures' which appear and are there to be observed. Hence the name 'phenomenology' and also the claim that the method is indeed objective. Zeal for this objectivity, moreover, promotes the demand, not only for freedom from prejudgement but for a suspense of judgement throughout the inquiry. There is to be no intrusion of any such evaluation on the part of the observer. Thus Brede Kristensen, one of the pioneers of this method, dismissed the name, Comparative Religion, not only because it had come to mean a comparison of different religions, considered as 'large units', ranged side by side, as distinguished from a comparison cutting across traditional boundaries, but also because Comparative Religion had come to mean a comparison for determining the *value* of different religions, with some of them described as 'higher' religions. Any such evaluation is excluded by the phenomenologist. The values in which he is interested are those attached by believers themselves to what they do and say.[1]

But here we have another requirement of this method, and while it is one which they may very well approve, it leads critics to question the claim to objectivity. It is the requirement for 'empathy' or fellow feeling with other believers. In saying that the values to be considered are the values which believers themselves attribute to their practices and beliefs, the phenomenologist goes on to say that this involves something more than mere description of what is said and done in the name of religion; it involves *understanding*, and understanding means empathy. If there

1. W. Brede Kristensen, *The Meaning of Religion*, tr. by John B. Carman, The Hague, 1960, pp. 1–13.

is to be any understanding or appreciation of the significance of what is happening in this living world of religion, something more is needed than the cold scrutiny which might be appropriate in a museum. There must be an imaginative entry into this realm. The student must see himself as mingling with the companies of believers, in their midst, trying to see what they may see, and, maybe, more than they may see. Gerardus van der Leeuw compares him with a landscape painter. He refers to the *art* of empathy and Dr Kraemer follows suit with the statement that 'good phenomenology is not primarily a method but an art'.[1]

Thus the scientific approach to the study of religion proposed a century ago is now supplemented by that of the artist, with all that the artist may put into it by way of an imaginative entry, as the need is seen for an understanding which goes beyond mere description. At the same time it is claimed that the study is still factual and the approach is still objective, which may be taken to mean that the interpretative, philosophic approach is here still excluded. But Gerardus van der Leeuw, it may be noted, describes the phenomenology of religion as a bridge between the sciences of religion and the philosophy of religion, and this may be construed to mean that the phenomenologist has at least gone half-way towards interpretation. He can, indeed, be seen as doing more than build a bridge. He has built a mill. In the process of selecting and presenting 'structures' of belief and practice he has taken the raw material of religious phenomena and shaped the forms of it so that their significance may be more apparent. In effect, he has told the philosopher what to observe, and, in doing so he has himself gone so far in the direction of interpretation that the question is raised: can there indeed be understanding

1. Hendrik Kraemer, in the Introduction to Brede Kristensen, op. cit., p. xi.

without interpretation?[1] Granted the admission of the artist's empathy, why not also grant the admission of the philosopher's judgement?

When these and similar questions are noted, it is not surprising to find new discussion today of what is required in the factual, comparative study of religion. Challenging the view that theologians and philosophers are disqualified by their allegiance to preconceived ideas, there is the argument that historians and others are all of them in similar case. None can pretend the cool objectivity of the computing machine.

As to the theologian, it is urged that his statements are the less likely to be misleading because his preconceived ideas are explicitly avowed. They are there in the open for all to see. He is not only the more on guard against obscuring prejudice himself; he puts others on guard by announcing his standpoint.

Second, it is urged that the objectivity of the computing machine is no more appropriate than it is possible when it comes to that due appraisal of the various and subtle ways in which men and women may express the faith which moves them. A study which is, whatever else, a study *of* people *by* people, demands all the intelligence and insight, as well as the empathy and imagination of which human nature is capable. When the spotlight is thus turned from the observer himself to what he has to observe, need appears for all the particular standpoints and approaches which can be shown to be relevant. They constitute, as it were, different vantage points from which some may be able to discern what is hidden to others.

In similar vein, it is argued that all that pertains to the philosophic discipline is indeed very relevant. As Professor Lewis points out in Part Two of this volume, 'philosophy

1. cf. Hendrik Kraemer, *Religion and The Christian Faith*, London 1965, p. 51.

has played a very important part in the development of the great religions over a long period'. His reminder is timely. For if earlier students of religion tended to concentrate on the intellectual elements and the more explicit statements of belief, with narrow reference to religious ideas and systems, treating religion as if it were philosophy in the raw, this and no more, the pendulum today has swung to the opposite extreme, with so much said about religious emotions or religious institutions that attention is distracted from the important role of religious thought and the way in which the sages no less than the prophets have influenced religious behaviour. Religion is more than philosophy but it has very generally been partnered by philosophy.

Besides the question: how can there be understanding without interpretation? we have, then, the question: how can there be due appreciation of religious interpretation without some exercise of philosophic judgement? It may very well be asked, for example, whether suspense of judgement is either possible or appropriate in the study of Hindu religion. Can a reader really appreciate the philosophical issues presented in this tradition or 'understand' what they may mean to Hindus without some philosophical interest of his own, an interest which may lead him from time to time to nod his head in approval or disapproval, explaining: 'Yes, this is true', or 'No, this is false'; 'Yes, this is valid', or 'No, this is contradictory'?

With these and kindred questions in mind, a good many today would conclude that the fence between factual and 'philosophical' studies of religion proposed in the interests of a scientific, objective approach was ill-conceived. They see no reason why a student should ask his factual questions in one class-room and move into another room for his philosophy of religion. Others would disagree. All said and done, they would insist, we have here two disciplines, each with its own particular requirements and purpose. The philosopher is expected to come in judgement. It is part of his purpose to separate the chaff of dubious religious statements from the wheat of reasonable conclusions. He thus may remove from the account a good deal which may be there at the start. Not so the historian. He must present the account as he finds it, with beliefs and practices which come into view, whether he privately approves them or not. While it may be allowed that the development of the scientific approach to the study of religion calls for some review of the relation between comparative studies and the philosophy of religion, there remain two disciplines, each with its own appropriate methods, and the historian must still be free from the leading strings of the philosopher.

It remains to be seen, however, whether philosophers today are either prepared or disposed to provide any leading strings.

Passing to the other side of the fence to observe what has been happening among the philosophers, one thing that may strike us at the outset is fragmentation of philosophic opinion today. During the century philosophers, no less than historians, have been on the move, and they have been moving in very different directions. Reference to philosophy a hundred years ago meant reference to certain dominant metaphysical systems. It was largely for this reason, as we have seen, that philosophers were regarded as coming a close second to theologians as authors of widely accepted doctrine which might prejudice scientific inquiry. It was still the Hegelian age. To say that all philosophers were marching in step would, of course, be going too far. Philosophers in any age very seldom march in step. Besides the whale of Hegelian idealism which was ready to swallow the Jonah of religion there was the Positivism which refused both the whale and Jonah. But the circle of the spellbound was large enough in each case to prompt comparison with theological circles.

As we have seen, the subsequent evolutionary philosophy was similarly fascinating. The same might be said of Whitehead's philosophy and Edmund Husserl's philosophical phenomenology nearer our own day. But none of the later philosophers had quite the same following as their predecessors. The philosophic world was, indeed, throughout the century becoming more and more a divided world. This is very much the situation today. In a recent survey Professor José Ferrater Mora, after emphasizing the present 'anarchy' of philosophical systems, names the following 'trends' which may be observed at the present time –

... idealism, personalism, realism, new realism, critical realism, realistic philosophy, immanentism, evolutionism, emergentism, pragmatism, intellectualism, operationism, intuitionism, irrationalism, rationalism, phenomenology, existentialism, logical positivism, logical empiricism, scientific empiricism, analytic philosophy, 'neutralism', Marxism, and Neo Scholasticism.[1]

Professor Mora adds that these examples are far from being exhaustive. He notes that 'as philosophical opinion is pulverized' definitions of philosophy abound more and more. Philosophy is also broken up into disciplines and sub-disciplines, with some thinkers putting all the emphasis on logic, others on theories of knowledge, and others on metaphysics. 'We can thus say practically anything we like about philosophy.'

Thus, while philosophy may still be warily regarded as something which threatens a scientific approach to religion by the encouragement of 'doctrines fixed in advance' the threat is reduced by the fact that there are so many doctrines

1. José Ferrater Mora, *Philosophy Today*, New York, 1960, p.65.

to choose from. There is no one dominating school presenting a world view which all reasonable men are disposed to accept. It can scarcely be said today that historians of religion are tempted to go with the crowd as far as philosophy is concerned, for there is here no crowd to go with.

In this respect, the divided world of philosophy is in sharp contrast to the theological world where there has been a remarkable consolidation of opinion especially in Protestant circles, largely due to the influence of Karl Barth and his camp followers. It is mainly from this quarter that we have the proposal for a study of religions in the light of avowed Christian premises. It is, however, a proposal associated with a 'Biblical realism' which distinguishes between the Biblical announcement itself and what the theologians have made of it, thus prompting a continuous scrutiny of any 'doctrine fixed in advance', Christian or otherwise.

As to the philosophers, the nearest approach to a doctrine fixed in advance which might be regarded as threatening free enterprise in the study of religion is the Verification Principle proposed by the logical positivists. It is indeed a principle which, at least in its earlier formulation, would seem to put an end to any enterprise at all in the study of religion, or any philosophical interest in the subject, for it presents tests of what may be accepted as meaningful which are so wedded to what may be seen through the senses alone that those who accept this principle are led to reject a great many religious statements as nonsense. On the other hand, the logical positivist may be seen as removing or reducing any threat to free enterprise in the study of religion which might come from philosophical quarters advancing other doctrines, since many of these are also rejected as meaningless. He is suspicious not only of religious statements but of the metaphysical statements made in his own domain of philosophy. He suggests indeed that they have no business there at all.

Generally speaking, philosophy through the ages has meant speculation concerning the nature of reality and hence a rash of metaphysical statements. But this is not how the logical positivist sees the function of philosophy. He excludes any metaphysical speculation, and, in this respect, he has the considerable company of a growing number of philosophers today who are engaged in what is comprehensively named analytical philosophy. It is a term used with reference to so many different positions that any general statement is subject to qualification when it comes to this or that particular writer but it can be said generally that the analysts are primarily concerned with the structure and expression of thought. They attempt no world view. They analyse the way in which people may talk *about* the world rather than the world itself. Critical of all vague, confused statements which seem to come out of the mists and get lost in the mists, they are, many of them, disposed to include religious statements in this category.

Nevertheless there has emerged from this school an interest in religious language which may be seen as bringing philosophers and students of religion together, promoting maybe a new kind of philosophy of religion requiring acquaintance both with philosophic disciplines and the field of comparative studies. When, for instance, Professor Ninian Smart asks what the Hindu teacher means when he says, 'Brahman is all this', is Professor Smart writing as a philosopher, or as a student of comparative religion, or as both? His philosophical training, it may be replied, leads him to put the question while his answer largely depends upon his competence in the history of religions.

This same philosophical scrutiny of religious language may lead the student of religions to look with new interest at what is being done in the realm of philosophy, persuaded that in this respect at least the philosopher has much to offer. A study of paradoxical language, for example, throws light on what the paradoxical statements of belief in nirvana signify to Buddhists.

The question arises, however, as to what the historian of religion may offer the philosopher beyond some examples of language, meaningless or meaningful, which the philosopher may welcome without entertaining any special interest in religion itself. For full answer to this question, however, there is need to observe that the philosophical analysts have not yet taken possession of the whole field of philosophy nor have they persuaded all who are engaged in this field that the only function of philosophy is to help people to avoid nonsense. There are still those who maintain that the metaphysical quest is a legitimate quest and a quest, moreover, which is not to be deterred by the imposition of principles of verification, principles which may be seen themselves to depend on metaphysical assumptions. It may indeed be the function of philosophers to help people to say what they mean. But this, it is argued, is not their only function. When all is said and done about the ways in which people may say what they mean there remains the larger question of what there is to say. Men are considerably less than human if they do not ask, explicitly or implicitly, what it means to be human, what are the conditions of human life, its total environment, its possibilities and its prospects. That they are still indeed very much human and still putting these questions is evident from much that is written today by playwrights, novelists, poets, scientists and others. There is still need, it is argued, for the philosopher whose task it is to put these piecemeal views together attempting a synoptic, unified view. If such an attempt takes him beyond physics, then so be it, metaphysician he must be, accepting the hazards as others have done in the venerable tradition to which he belongs.

Where there is such argument – and there are signs today of its renewed vitality – we may expect a philosopher to turn to religion, as he turns to science, art and history, for grist for his philosophical mills. And when it comes to religion he will not be content merely to note how or when and where a thing has been said. He will be concerned with *what* has been said, with its significance, its value, its truth. There will be here no question of any suspense of judgement. On the contrary, it will be seen as part of the philosophical scrutiny to discriminate and evaluate and pass judgement in the light of reason. In other words, there will be philosophy of religion after the older model: a philosophical, rational, appraisal of religious beliefs and practices.

What, then, has the historian of religions to offer in regard to such an engagement? Does the philosopher need the historian at his elbow when he comes to discuss religion?

Thus far we have had in review what has been happening in the world of philosophy in general but here we must turn to philosophy of religion in particular, for answers to our questions depend very largely on what is regarded as pertinent to a philosopher's religious interest and what is pertinent in the discipline of philosophy of religion, since a distinction should be drawn between religious philosophy and philosophy of religion. In the first case, there is clearly no telling the philosopher where he should start or to whom he should refer if he wants to think religiously any more than there is a telling of the prophet, the poet, the tinker, or the shoemaker. All that can be claimed is that his thought may be stimulated by acquaintance with comparative religion and what the historian in this field may present.

In the case of the philosophy of religion, however, a good

deal more can be said. Here a reference to what has actually been said and done in the name of religion is obviously relevant if what is proposed is a scrutiny of religious statements made by others rather than an adventure in religious thought pursued by the philosopher from whatever premises he may prefer. In this case one may expect a special concern to ascertain in all ways possible the origin, context and purport of religious statements. It is here that the historian has indeed much to offer.

In the first place he invites reference to a wider canvas than might otherwise be contemplated. As pursued in the West, the philosophy of religion has hitherto been largely concerned with issues presented within the Judaic-Christian tradition and the tradition of Greek thought. More recent discussion of these issues has been stimulated and informed by increasing reference to other contexts of religious beliefs following the growing western acquaintance with the traditions of the Orient, especially the Hindu and Buddhist traditions. A philosophy of religion against the full background of world religions, however, has still to be developed. And such a philosophy will be subject to continued revision on the part of western writers for at least two reasons.

There is first of all the fact that the religions thus brought into view are living religions. As in the case of the Christian tradition, they present new movements of thought, new insights and new challenges, especially in this present day when the different religions are stimulated by closer encounter, one with another.

There is secondly the fact that the western study of oriental religions is still a comparatively young study. It is constantly being informed by new knowledge, such as the new knowledge of the great Hindu tradition provided by recent archaeological discoveries in North India. As will be shown in the chapters which follow, such new knowledge has meant reappraisal by western writers of all the religious traditions which they have studied. Moreover, this same reappraisal has been prompted, not only by new knowledge, but by new understanding which has come with the development of new approaches to the subject during the past century. In any inquiry, much depends on what the observer may be looking for and the directions taken. As compared with students at the beginning of the century, when attention was focused on the exciting new texts from the Orient which were being brought to the West, with principal reference to terms and ideas presented in these texts, students today find themselves engaged in a much wider range of inquiry, as well as what might be described as an inquiry in depth. Studies of primitive religion, for instance, where no texts or scriptures are forthcoming, have meant increasing regard for the significance of what believers may do, including the rites in which they engage, besides the significance of what they say. Nor is this wider regard confined to the study of primitive religion. It informs the study of traditions where texts and scriptures *are* available. Professor Zwi Werblowsky, for example, suggests that 'one may get nearer to the heart of Catholicism by attending Mass than by reading theological manuals' and adds that much the same applies in the case of Judaism. All told, there is today a much more extensive reference to the various ways, often indirect and far from explicit, by which men and women may express the faith by which they live, and hence an inquiry which is at once more subtle and more searching. The Hinduism known to scholars today is a very different Hinduism from that presented by earlier western scholars, and the Hinduism presented tomorrow may be different again from that portrayed today.

To note this progress in scholarship is surely to conclude that it has a very definite bearing on that regard for contexts which philosophers would be the first to emphasize.

If there is need to read religious statements, no less than others, in the light of their contexts, there is equal need for true conception of these contexts. It is perhaps in this respect that the close relation between the two disciplines, philosophy of religion and the history of religions, is most evident.

As to any conceivable fence between these two disciplines, our glance at what has been happening on the philosophers' side of the fence points to much the same conclusion as that which was reached in regard to the historians: whatever distinction may be drawn between the methods and purposes of the two disciplines, it should not be one which ignores or obstructs that frequent passage from the one discipline to the other which full discussion of the subject of religion invites.

The general reader may be more persuaded of the force of this conclusion than the expert blinded by his own special interests, for he will probably approach the subject with both historical and philosophical questions in mind, interested in the whence and how of religious statements, the contexts in which they appear and the history behind them, but not less interested in the issues they present, in the significance of these statements and the bearing they may have on his own conception of life and grasp of truth.

The present volume assumes this two-fold interest.

Part One is written from the standpoint of a historian of religions. This present chapter is followed by three chapters which may be regarded as constituting an introduction to the wider background of religious life and thought which historians are presenting today. In a treatment which is necessarily selective, it has been considered appropriate to concentrate on the three great living religions, Hinduism, Buddhism and Islam since the new and growing acquaintance with these three traditions has been one of the main influences in stimulating modern philosophical discussions of religion in the West. In each case, as will be shown, this growing acquaintance has meant the reappraisal to which reference has been made in this chapter.

This historical treatment of the subject is followed by a philosophical treatment in Part Two in the form of an essay which demonstrates some of the ways in which philosophy, most of all in the forms which are dominant in the West today, is relevant to the study of religions.

11

The Hindu Tradition

HINDU, which simply means Indian, is an adjective which has been used to refer to what has been believed and practised by some four hundred million people and their forebears for some five thousand years, none of whom refer to any one single teacher acknowledged by all or recite any one creed accepted by all. Taken as a whole, the Hindu tradition is one of the oldest religious traditions in the world. But it is exceedingly difficult to take it as a whole, for it is also one of the most diversified religious traditions in the world. It is a great Ganges River of religious beliefs and practices fed by many streams.

About all that can be said with reference to this great tradition, 'taken as a whole', is that we are here dealing with a tradition arising on Indian soil and largely confined to India. But even this broad statement is subject to qualification. India has known other traditions, including Christianity and Islam. And what is called Hinduism is today being spread abroad beyond the shores of India, with the claim that Hindu teachings are of universal interest.

Some distinctive features of Hindu religion, however, may be named, such as the caste system and the concept of Absolute Brahman. There are also certain basic assumptions which must be known before there can be any kind of understanding of the Hindu outlook. Among these basic ideas is the view of life indicated by the term *samsara* (migration) which means that the Hindu is far from thinking, as do most people in the West, that his life began with his birth on this planet. On the contrary, he thinks of this present span of life as only one in a succession of lives, taking various forms, not all of them human and not all of them lived on this earth. He also thinks in terms of a vast

31

universe including other realms inhabited by men or gods or both. Another basic idea is the idea of *karma* which denotes the conception of moral causation, a conception which means that what a man is and where he is today is largely determined by what he has done in many yesterdays with regard to *dharma* (sacred, eternal law). Along with these conceptions there is the conception of salvation named by the term *moksha*, which signifies emancipation from the bonds of present existence. To attain this emancipation it is necessary to transcend *avidya* (ignorance) or *maya* (illusion).

Even in the case of these distinctive features, however, there is again need for qualification. It cannot be taken for granted that any one of these basic ideas has been held from the beginning of this great tradition any more than it can be taken for granted that the distinctive Hindu caste system has existed from the beginning. Most scholars today see these conceptions and associated practices emerging at various times in the course of India's long history. A good many of them would use the term Hinduism, if they use it at all, with limited reference to views and practices which are not clearly established until near the beginning of the Christian era, that is, about half-way in the full story of this venerable tradition. Our list of basic conceptions would be, indeed, a very misleading introduction if it left the impression that Hindu thought and life can be adequately mapped or summarized in such a way.

Any notion of the kind is immediately dissipated when we turn to Hindu scripture. First, there are the Vedas (Veda meaning knowledge or wisdom). These are texts written during the course of some fifteen hundred or two thousand years before the Christian era. We may begin with the *Rig Veda*, the collection of hymns addressed to the gods introduced by the Aryan invaders who swept into India at the beginning of this period – hymns to Indra, the god of war and storm; to Varuna, the universal ruler and guardian of the law (*dharma*); to Agni, god of fire; and many others, most of them now forgotten. Included in the Vedas there are prose texts dealing with sacrificial rituals (*Brahmanas*) and later, the more philosophical texts, the *Upanisads*. The Vedic texts thus constitute what might be called a bible of primary scriptures, *sruti* (that which is heard).

In addition, however, there is a second body of authoritative scripture, *smriti* (that which is remembered) which includes the great Hindu epics, the *Mahabharata* and the *Ramayana*, manuals and law books such as the *Code of Manu*, the eighteen major *Puranas* and the eighteen minor *Puranas*. The *Puranas* alone amount to a vast mass of sacred literature full of stories and legends with popular appeal.

The western reader is not helped in his attempt to understand this wide range of scripture and what it means to the Hindu mind by the fact that some of the terms used are variously employed. The word Veda, for example, is often used with narrow reference to the earlier texts only. The term Vedanta (literally, the end of the Veda) may refer broadly to the teaching given in the later texts, the *Upanisads* or, more narrowly, to a system of philosophy based on these texts. There is also the fact that the sacred texts reflect changes of thought and even opposing trends of thought which are confusing. Many of the gods mentioned in the *Rig Veda* disappear from view by the end of the Vedic period. In the later Vedic texts the main trend of thought is neither polytheistic nor theistic but in the direction of a pantheistic monism, with reference to Absolute Brahman, while in the epic scriptures the trend is theistic, with reference to the high gods Visnu and Siva, who, together with the god Brahma (*not* Absolute Brahman), later constitute what is sometimes called the Hindu trinity. But this reference to a Hindu trinity may again be misleading because there is nothing in Hindu thought which corresponds to the central conception of a Christian Trinity.

The Hindu respect for sacred scripture is indicated by Dr Sarma's view that one reason why Buddhism lost its hold in India was the Buddhist 'substitution of individual reason for the authority of the Vedas as a guide in religious matters'.[1] Dr Sarma also says, as do others, that all the orthodox schools of Hinduism accept this scriptural authority and guidance. But when we consider how vast is the body of this scripture, how varied its contents, and the consequent elasticity of its guidance, it is not surprising to find reference to no less than twelve schools which are described as orthodox, nor is it surprising to find these schools varying from the Sankhya dualism which names no god, to the nondualistic (*advaita*) school of Sankara presenting a qualified belief in god which is rejected by the resolute theist, Ramanuja, as no belief in god at all.

Some historians find it convenient to name four main periods, first the early period of Vedic polytheism, second, the Vedantist period with its monistic expositions of Absolute Brahman, third, a period beginning about 200 B.C. and continuing through most of the Christian era notable for its development of *bhakti* devotional theism, and lastly the modern period responsive to western influence. But Hindu history bursts the seams of any such pattern.

All told, any attempt at a brief introductory outline must end with the admission that no such outline has been presented but rather a confusing medley of intersecting lines. Nor can it be otherwise in the case of this venerable, rich, baffling, often surprising and frequently elusive tradition named Hinduism. What confronts us is a complexity as challenging as it is baffling, which refuses to be

1. D. S. Sarma, 'The Nature and History of Hinduism', *The Religion of the Hindus*, ed. Morgan, p. 32.

fitted into any small pigeon-hole of the mind, if such there be.

The most distinctive feature of Hindu or Indian religion is indeed its vast complexity. Hindu writers at the present time are among the first to emphasize this complexity as they note how hard it is to see the wood for the trees and avoid taking some of the trees as all that constitutes the wood. A similar sensitivity to this same complexity distinguishes western views today.

It means a very different view of Hindu life and thought from that which obtained a century ago. A good many of the earlier western writers drew a sharp line between what was called philosophical Hinduism and popular Hinduism. Philosophical or sophisticated Hinduism was then presented with narrow reference to the dominant school associated with the medieval scholar-saint, Sankara, the Thomas Aquinas of Hindu thought, which was described as monistic or pantheistic. In contrast, popular Hinduism was seen as polytheistic gathered around a superstitious respect for some of the many gods in the Hindu pantheon. Accompanying this hasty classification there was a special regard for the more philosophical or systematic presentations of Hindu thought to the comparative neglect of the poetic expressions of the Hindu view of life which can be found in the great epics. There was also a very western separation of philosophy from religion which is foreign to the Indian mind.

Today, with increasing knowledge of the many and various sources which have to be taken into account for anything approaching a more adequate understanding of the great, broad, immensely diversified Hindu tradition, we find it said that when it comes to Indian religion we must see it in terms, not of any one religion, whether called Hindu or not, but in terms of several religions, if indeed our western concept of religion is at all applicable in this context. In particular, there is growing regard for the *bhakti* tradition which presents a devotional, theistic interpretation challenging the monistic tendencies of Hindu thought.

A further reason for reappraisal in this respect has been the recent discovery of what has been called the 'Harappa religion' or the Indus Valley religion. Historians of an earlier generation began their account of Hinduism with the coming of the robust Aryans, light-skinned nomads of Indo-European stock who swept into India through the northwest mountain passages in the second millenium B.C., subduing the dark-skinned Dravidian inhabitants and introducing a pantheon of gods as robust as themselves. In our own day, however, archaeological excavations in the Indus Valley have led the more imaginative writers to picture a civilization between the cities of Mohenjo-Dāro and Harappa which flourished long before the coming of the Aryans, and even cautious scholars agree that cults such as the worship of the terrible mother goddess Durga or Kali, the consort of Siva, which survive in India today, can be traced back to the religion of this pre-Aryan period. Figurines of naked or half-naked women found by the archaeologists suggest such a cult. Other features of later Hinduism such as the phallus worship associated with the god Siva may also be traced back to this earlier period.

If there is need in general, then, to revise earlier accounts of the great religious traditions of the world in the light of new knowledge, this is manifestly true in regard to the Hindu religion. Nor have we reached an end to such revision. For besides the fact that we have here to deal with the rich variety of faith and practice which has developed in a vast sub-continent during the course of a very long history, there is the fact that Hindus today are, as an Indian Christian observer has put it, 'strangely alive as Hindus' – alive both to the richness of their heritage and the challenges of the modern world. Hindus are also addressing the world at large as seldom if ever before in their history. Exponents of the Hindu view of life such as India's distinguished philosopher-statesman, Dr S. Radhakrishnan, are seeking not only to engage western interest but to remove western misconceptions. Hindu writers have also produced revised statements of their faith. Sri Aurobindo, for example, widely regarded as one of the greatest thinkers of modern India with a following which has continued since his death in 1950, certainly wrote from within the Hindu tradition but his version of the Hindu view of life reflects his familiarity with modern western thought.

One way and another, then, there is abundant occasion and need for reappraisal. To be confronted with Hinduism is immediately to be confronted with the need emphasized in our introduction for reconsidering earlier western views of oriental religion. The need is especially patent in the case of Hindu thought since it is still identified in the minds of a good many western readers with monistic or pantheistic trends, trends which are undoubtedly there but which by no means constitute the full context. If such pantheistic trends are emphasized to the exclusion of all else, we may very well wonder how it is that some Hindus today are so insistent that they believe just as firmly and intelligently in a personal god as do Christians and others.

It may also be noted that this reappraisal is informed not only by new knowledge such as the Indus Valley discoveries but by new approaches in the study of religion which take fuller account of what may be signified by what Hindus do besides what they may say than was the case in earlier studies. This same reappraisal, however, with its better informed regard for the complexity of Indian thought and life, makes it the more difficult to know where to begin in an introduction which must at least aim at eliciting some of the principal issues raised in this tradition.

In this situation it is fortunate that we can turn to one particular Hindu scripture, the *Bhagavad Gita* or the *Song of the Lord* which, more than any other sacred text, informs Hindu thought and conduct. No scripture is more widely read in India today. There is also the fact that the *Bhagavad Gita* is regarded by a great many scholarly Hindus as bringing together all that is most significant in their tradition. It has indeed been variously interpreted, for commentary after commentary has been written on the *Gita* and the opinions have ranged from the view that the thought of the *Gita* is essentially monistic to the view that its main and final emphasis on the *bhakti* approach makes the *Gita* 'a new gospel, not hitherto proclaimed in India, the gospel of the love of God for man'.[1] Whatever conclusions may be drawn, however, to read the *Gita* is certainly to be introduced to some of the main themes of Hindu thought as well as to some of the main practices of Hindu life. It is also to be introduced to Hindu poetry as well as Hindu prose, for the *Gita* is part of the great *Mahabharata* epic and it begins with a chapter from the story of the grim, fratricidal war which is told in that epic.

As presented in the *Bhagavad Gita* it is a story which rings very true to life, the story of a warrior who asks desperate questions as many another soldier has done about the apparent call to duty which bids him kill or be killed. The scene is the great battlefield of Kurekshetra, the warrior is Arjuna and the companion to whom he puts his questions is the god, Krisna, who is the high god Visnu, come to Arjuna's aid in the human guise of his charioteer.

What is the sense of such a war? asks Arjuna desperately—

I can't stand, my mind is reeling. Here are my very own kinsmen so eager to fight each other. What possible good can

1. R. C. Zaehner, *Hinduism*, London, 1963, p. 122.

come of it all? I may be killed or I may conquer. But all the
kingdoms in the world are not worth such a price. Think of
all that war means, all the passions aroused and all that follows
– the confusion, the lawlessness, the corruption, the destruc-
tion of families and homes.

Arjuna sinks down on the seat of his chariot, casting away
his bow and arrow, overwhelmed by his despair. 'I will not
fight' he exclaims.[1]

The fact that the *Gita* begins in this way, turning the
spotlight on human experience, points immediately to the
equation between truth and experience which is one of
the features of Hindu thought. Indian philosophy, says Dr
Radhakrishnan, is rooted in experience and he defines religion, which to the Indian mind is so closely akin to philosophy, as 'life experienced in its depth' adding that 'beliefs
are codified expressions of experience'.[2] For the Hindu,
the way of salvation is the way of knowledge, but what is
sought is not knowledge *about* reality but knowledge *of*
reality; a knowledge which is awareness; a knowledge by
acquaintance. Hence an emphasis on intuition and the
fact that Hindu sages are significantly described as those
who *see* the truth. It is largely because of this emphasis on
what each must experience for himself that Hindus are so
critical of the intolerance which derives from an attachment to dogmas, which, they say, are then substituted for
the realization of truth. In keeping with this emphasis, Sri
Aurobindo comments that the *Gita* must be the fruit of a
profound spiritual experience. Nothing less could account
for its wisdom.[3] Here we have something which immediately quickens western interest. It obviously challenges
the western disposition to dogmatic attitudes, grounded in

1. *Bhagavad Gita*, I (paraphrased).
2. S. Radhakrishnan, *Indian Philosophy*, Vol. I, London, 1923, p.32;
Freedom of the Spirit, Cambridge, Mass., 1960, p. 6.
3. Sri Aurobindo Ghose, *Essays on the Gita*, New York, 1950.

a respect for creedal statements. There is further challenge in the fact that Hindu thinkers appear to regard their appeal to experience as very much part of the strength of their position, whereas some in the West may see it as a weakness. The Hindu emphasis may be held to support the conclusion that religious statements amount to no more than an expression of human emotions, telling us much about how human beings confront their world but little about the world itself. Others, however, may find the Hindu analysis much more subtle and some of the features of this analysis may lead them to criticize their own tendency to reduce religious beliefs to mere expressions of human emotion. The appeal to experience in the *Bhagavad Gita*, however, is chiefly emphasized by the dramatic quality of the short introductory scene, with the intensely human Arjuna pictured against a vivid background of imminent battle – conches and kettle-drums, tabors and horns blaring forth in tumultuous noise, banners waving, the foe drawn up in battle order, eager for the strife of war, and Arjuna and Krisna looking across at them from a chariot yoked to white horses. Beyond this introduction, there is little further narrative. From now on the centre of the stage is taken by the god Krisna and the greater part of the *Gita* consists of Krisna's instruction, although we are reminded of Arjuna's continued presence, and the agitated concern to which this instruction is addressed, by Arjuna's interjected comments and further questions, until we come to a central scene when Arjuna the warrior is again very much before us, as in all his astonished humanity, he shrinks back from the very vision which he has demanded.

Meantime there is Krisna's sober instruction, an instruction which is regarded by Hindus as threading together in what Dr Radhakrishnan describes as 'brilliant synthesis'[1], currents of religious and philosophical thought

1. S. Radhakrishnan, *The Bhagavad Gita*, New York, 1948, p. 15.

which were competing with each other at the time the *Gita* was written (probably in the third or fourth century B.C.): the Vedic cult of sacrifice, the scriptural conception of transcendent Brahman, the Sankhya dualism, the Yoga meditation, and the theistic conceptions of the *bhakti* tradition.

Krisna's first word to the desperate Arjuna refers the reader to the most distinctive feature of Hindu society: the caste system. Arjuna is exhorted not to yield to an ignoble unmanliness which is unworthy of a warrior.[1] A few verses later this admonition is amplified. For the warrior caste 'there exists no greater good than a war enjoined by duty': such a war is 'an open door to heaven'.[2]

Much is written today that gives the impression that the caste system is entirely discredited in modern India and on the way out. This, however, is doubtful. Westerners may find it hard to reconcile the caste system with democratic trends in the India of today, as indeed do some Hindus themselves, for the caste system makes short shrift of any notion of equal status or equal opportunity. The nearest approach to the Hindu caste system is the western feudal system which separated the nobility from the serfs. But even in the feudal system there were at least a few serfs who became knights, while no low caste Hindu has ever become a brahmin – not, at least, in this present life. One is born into one's caste and one must stay in one's caste until death, when indeed there is possibility of change, if, and only if, one has fulfilled the duties pertinent to one's caste, as the low caste *sudras* are reminded in the *Laws of Manu*: '[A *sudra* who is] pure, the servant of his betters . . . attains [in his next life] a higher caste.'[3] But never in this present life. Even if his master frees him from his service, he remains a servant for he cannot get away from his own inner nature

1. *Bhagavad Gita* II, 3. 2. ibid., II, 31 ff.
3. *The Laws of Manu*, 335.

which means servitude.[1] The regulations for the higher castes affect almost every aspect of life, prescribing what one must wear, what work one must do and whom one may marry; what food one may eat and who may prepare it; and the religious duties one should perform.

Originally there were four castes, the *brahmin* caste (the priests), the *kshatryas* (the warrior and ruling caste), the *vaisyas* (farmers and traders), and the *sudras* (the labourers). But the system has mushroomed until today there are some three thousand castes and sub-castes in India.

The view that the caste system is doomed has been fostered by an opinion, accepted by some Hindus themselves, that caste in the first place had very little to do with religious belief; it is rather to be explained in terms of racial division as the conquering Aryans vanquished the Dravidians and put them to work in the fields, or in terms of economic convenience.

Caste, indeed, is one of the aspects of Hinduism on which there are a great many second thoughts today. But it is going too far to ignore the religious factor altogether. Whatever may have been the origin of the system it has come to have strong religious sanctions behind it. Besides referring to the passages in the *Gita* and the *Laws of Manu*, Hindus may refer to one of the Vedic creation hymns which posits the brahmin caste as coming from the mouth of the primal Being (*Purusha*), the warrior caste coming from his arms, the farmer caste coming from his thighs and the menials coming from his feet.[2]

What, perhaps, most influences the Hindu attitude to caste is the association with the belief in transmigration and the consequent conviction that one's birth in this or that caste is determined by qualities of character developed in previous lives. Thus, in the *Gita*, the reference to Arjuna's caste duty as a warrior is followed almost im-

1. ibid., 414.　　2. *Rig Veda*, X, 90.

mediately by a reference to the belief in transmigration. Arjuna is told that he may indeed be slain. But all that will be slain is his body. As worn out garments are exchanged for new garments, so man may expect to 'take on other bodies that are new'.[1]

It has already been observed that belief in transmigration governs the whole Hindu outlook on life. But it is worth pausing again to note, from this *Gita* passage, how this is so, for if there is one thing more than another which distinguishes the religions born on Indian soil – Buddhism no less than Hinduism – from the family of western religions, it is this belief in rebirth. The belief is held so firmly that it is more often regarded as a fact than a belief.

Krisna, however, has something more in mind than transmigration. He is moving towards the great theme of nearly all schools of Hindu thought, however much they may differ in other respects: the theme that man must lay hold on that eternal life which is indestructible and imperishable, and, piercing through all misleading appearances and confusions, see himself, his true, his real self, in terms of this eternal life. Then, indeed, the warrior, no less than others, and on the very field of battle where death threatens, will know that, in final analysis, there is no death or only death as the gateway to life –

Weapons do not cleave this self, fire does not burn him. . . . He is uncleavable, He cannot be burnt. . . . He is eternal, all pervading.[2]

The reference here is to the Sankhya Philosophy with its emphasis on the self (*purusha*), pure consciousness and the immortal spirit in man which must be distinguished from the material and the bodily and realized as the true self if there is to be liberation (*moksha*). In other words, Krisna begins (for this is the real starting point of his instruction)

1. ibid., X, 90.   2. *Bhagavad Gita*, II, 23–4.

with the need for true knowledge about the self. Man must cut through the jungle of delusion.[1] He must not be led astray by the roving senses.[2] He must know that which is indestructible and what is declared of 'the eternal embodied [soul]'.[3]

The jungle of delusion? It is often held that Hindu thought in general reduces human life to no more than a dream and a bad dream at that, dismissing the world as unreal, as the sleeper is invited to awake and find himself in the only world which is real, the realm of the eternal. Sankara's use of the ambiguous term *maya* (not the term used in this *Gita* passage) may perhaps suggest this. But even if Sankara does go so far, his philosophy, although widely accepted, is not the only Hindu philosophy. As to any dismissal of the world as unreal, it may be noted that a good many Hindu writers are at pains to say that the familiar illustration of the rope which appears to be a snake does not mean that because there is, in fact, no snake, there is nothing at all: there is the rope.

It cannot be denied that Hindu discussions of the jungle of delusion raise questions in the minds of western readers including questions regarding the significance of ethical decision. What, for instance, are we to make of the verse in this *Gita* passage which suggests that if Arjuna has the right mental attitude he will 'leave behind in this world both good and evil deeds'?[4] Arjuna has raised a definitely ethical question: Is it right to kill? The *dharma* of the caste system tells him that it is indeed right for him to kill. That is his plain duty as a warrior. But Krisna's first reference to this *dharma* of caste does not convince Arjuna. He persists: 'I'll not fight.'[5] Is he in effect appealing to a higher *dharma* than that of caste, and is he now being told that if he really

1. ibid., II, 52.   2. ibid., II, 57.
3. ibid., II, 18.   4. ibid., II, 50.
5. ibid., II, 59.

discerns this higher *dharma*, really 'sees the highest'[1] he will transcend all such ethical distinctions? Or does the suggestion that good and evil deeds can be left behind simply mean, as some Hindu writers suggest, that the man who is free from delusion and has the right mental attitude is incapable of evil?[2]

It is not surprising that the reference to the jungle of delusion should come thus early in Krisna's instruction, for a reference of this kind is one of the starting points of all Hindu thought. Evil is virtually equated with ignorance or illusion. Sinful man is deceived man, man deceived by appearances. Salvation (*moksha*) is freedom from deception; it is the overcoming of delusion. The main purpose of Krisna's introductory instruction is to emphasize this. First there is the affirmation which is common to most Hindu schools and indeed to most religions – the affirmation of the primacy of the spiritual. Second, there is emphasis on the need for discipline (*yoga*) if Arjuna is to realize for himself the primacy of the spiritual. The term *yoga* which comes from the same root as the English word, *yoke*, has a double connotation. It means the discipline itself ('Take my yoke upon you') but it also refers to the goal of the discipline – the yoking or the union with Brahman which is the goal of all Hindu aspiration.

Three disciplines are presented in the *Gita*, the way of knowledge (*jnana*), the way of works (*karma*), and the way of devotion (*bhakti*). It may be held that Arjuna is offered his choice between these three ways. There is much in Hindu thought and practice to suggest such a choice. The different ways may be seen as appropriate to different innate capacities in man. Thus the way of knowledge may be regarded as the contemplative brahmin's natural way, while the way of works may be regarded as the active warrior's

1. ibid., II, 9.
2. cf. Radhakrishnan, *The Bhagavad Gita*, comment on II, 50, p. 121.

natural way. The way of *bhakti* may then be seen either as a way for a man who has neither the brahmin's intelligence nor the warrior's energy. But it may also be conceived as a way which is preferable to both the way of knowledge or the way of works.

Krisna's instruction to Arjuna, however, is perhaps better interpreted as holding all three ways together. Arjuna the warrior cannot avoid action. For that matter, no man can refuse the engagement of life: 'no one can remain, even for the moment, without doing work.'[1] But the goal cannot be realized by action in itself. All depends on the spirit in which a man acts, the spirit of disinterested, or dedicated action as against action from selfish motives. All depends, therefore, on the knowledge and motive informing his activity.

If the goal is union, yoking, with Brahman, then the discipline or disciplines proposed must be in accord with the conception or conceptions of Brahman. It is in this respect that the *Gita* is such a valuable introduction to Hindu thought for it presents two main conceptions of Brahman and holds them together as indeed they are held together in Hindu tradition. There is the more impersonal or suprapersonal conception of the Absolute Brahman, without attributes (*nirguna Brahman*), the ultimate reality which is 'not this, not that' (*neti neti*), transcending all human thought; a conception which reflects the monistic trends of Hindu thought. But there is also the more personal conception of Brahman developed in the *bhakti* theistic tradition (*saguna Brahman*), the Brahman whose attributes are the attributes of the personal Lord, Isvara, manifest in the high gods and their incarnate avatars. In the *Gita* the high god is Visnu and the avatar is Krisna.

It cannot be said, however, that in reading the *Gita* we are immediately aware of these two conceptions. For that

1. *Bhagavad Gita*, III, 5.

matter, it is not at all clear in the beginning that the *Gita* will deal with such a subject. In the introduction there is little hint of the great Vision which is to send the astonished Arjuna to his knees. The *Gita* does not begin with any such announcement. There is no question here of sudden vision nor of any complete doctrine flung in sharp answer to Arjuna's question. The *Gita* begins at the level of the question itself, not from the heights of heaven but very much from the confused earth where a confused man is simply asking: What shall I *do*? It begins by turning this question around until Arjuna is led to ask: What must I *be*? It proceeds at the sober level of the disciplines which he must consider until Arjuna is led to ask about the goal of such disciplines. With the naming of the goal, there is naming of union with Brahman and the question: Who is Brahman? arises.

The *Gita* is poetry and any analysis of it must respect this poetry. There is indeed philosophy behind it and the prose of the philosophy is interjected. But there is also behind it the rich mythology and symbolism of the Hindu tradition inviting, much of it, wonder rather than analysis. At the outset, however, this richness is held in reserve as also is the full vision of Brahman.

What we have is a gradual build up of thought towards this vision and an instruction which keeps pace with Arjuna's growing understanding of the full majesty of his instructor. At first, Arjuna is so unaware of this majesty that he can turn to Krisna and tell him to stop talking in riddles, 'with words that seem confused'.[1] Krisna is his charioteer, recognized sufficiently as a god to be asked for counsel, but as a god by man's side, god as avatar, in a human form which invites familiarity.

Arjuna's protest leads Krisna to explain the *yoga* of works (*karma*) in terms of the right understanding emphasized by

1. ibid., III, 2.

the *yoga* of knowledge, a right understanding which means dedicated activity of the kind exemplified in the pattern of Brahmanic sacrificial ritual. The conception of the divine here reflected is the Vedic conception of the high gods, worshipped by man and cooperating with man as he 'turns the wheel' of sacrificial action, joining in the activity which sustains the universe.[1] When Krisna speaks as if he himself was responsible for the deeper insights in this earlier Vedic teaching, Arjuna turns to him in surprise. Responsible for teaching given in past ages? Who, then, is this Krisna? It is here that we have the frequently quoted avatar verses, as Krisna unfolds the further conception of the divine which presents the Supreme Being as 'descending' in response to human need, coming to the side of man as he has now come in the form of Krisna to the side of Arjuna

> whenever there is a decline of righteousness
> For the protection of the good
> And for the destruction of evil-doers.[2]

But Arjuna still seems to take Krisna pretty much for granted, partly because the discussion remains at what the *Gita* itself calls a practical level,[3] with reference to the *yoga* discipline. It is only as Krisna emphasizes more and more that this practice must be rooted in faith that Arjuna is led to ask: What is the object of such faith? What is Brahman? Even so, he is still far from identifying Krisna himself as Brahman. 'What is Brahman, O best of men?'[4]

From now on the reference is increasingly to Brahman,

1. ibid., III, 15–16.   2. ibid., IV, 6, 7.

3. ibid., VII, 2. tr. F. Edgerton, Harvard University Press, 1944, *see* note, p. 181.

4. *Bhagavad Gita*, VIII, 1, 2. *purusottama*: Radhakrishnan translates: 'O best of persons.'

'that Supreme Divine Spirit',[1] pervading all the universe
in the form of the unmanifest,[2] sending forth again and
again the whole host of beings,[3] the father of this world,[4]
the object and lord of all worship,[5] the starting point of the
gods,[6] the origin of all,[7] the source of all understanding.[8]
As Krisna continues to say all this in the first person, including himself in the reference to Brahman, Arjuna is at
last led to exclaim:

> Thou [Krisna] art the Supreme Brahman!
> And thou declarest this to me.
> God of gods, lord of the world!
> O, tell me more, tell me in full detail.
> How am I to conceive Thee?
> I am listening to the nectar of Thy life-giving words.[9]

Krisna replies in terms which reflect the Vedanta statement:
'Brahman is all this.'[10]

> I am the soul abiding in the heart of all beings . . .
> I am Visnu . . . I am Indra . . . I am Siva . . . I am the ocean . . .
> I am the Ganges River . . . I am the Ordainer (Creator)
> with faces in all directions . . . I am death . . . I am
> the majesty of the majestic . . . the courage of the
> courageous . . . I support this entire world. . . .[11]

But does Arjuna yet understand? He says that he does. He
says that he is no longer bewildered. He knows now that
'nothing lives and moves apart from God'.[12] But if Arjuna
really understands would he make the daring request which
he now makes. He asks to see God, to see 'Thy form as
God, O supreme spirit'.[13]

1. ibid., VIII, 10.
2. ibid., IX, 4.
3. ibid., IX, 8.
4. ibid., IX, 17.
5. ibid., IX, 24.
6. ibid., X, 2.
7. ibid., X. 8.
8. ibid., X, 9 ff.
9. ibid., X, 12 ff.
10. *Brihadaranyaka Upanisad*, II, iv, 6.
11. *Bhagavad Gita*, X, 19 ff.
12. ibid., X, 39.
13. ibid., XI, 3.

Krisna's immediate reply might be taken as a warning. 'To see God! That is not for human eyes.' Nevertheless

> I give thee a supernatural eye:
> Behold My mystic power as God![1]

The light that now bursts upon the amazed Arjuna is more than the light of a thousand suns, a mass radiance, glowing on all sides, burning the whole universe. For the Brahman now revealed, whose face is as flaming fire, is Brahman the destroyer as well as Brahman the creator. He is the Brahman presented in the shattering imagery of Hindu symbolism, 'of many mouths and eyes, of many arms, thighs and feet, of many bellies, terrible with many tusks', devouring all the worlds, receiving between his flaming jaws the very warriors who now stand before Arjuna, ready for battle. He is Brahman, awful and terrible, the ultimate One, summoning Arjuna –

> Arise thou, win glory
> Conquer thine enemies
> Do thou slay [since] they are already slain by Me.[2]

Arjuna, then, is only an instrument! The fate of those who will be killed in the battle, observes a Hindu commentator, does not rest with Arjuna; it has been decided by acts committed long ago.

But Arjuna, for the moment, has now no thought for the battle or for anything else except this Form confronting him, this Form which he had known as Krisna, this Form which he had treated with such familiarity, this shattering, terrible Form which he has wished to see, this Ultimate Brahman. He is confounded. He is aghast at his own presumption. He stands with bowed head, in astonished awe. He prostrates himself, faltering –

> O Infinite Being, Lord of the gods . . .
> The Being and the non-being and beyond both.

1. ibid., XI, 8.   2. ibid., XI, 34.

. . . .

Homage be to Thee . . . Thou All.
Forgive me!
Forgive me for whatever I may have said rashly
Calling Thee Krisna, thinking of Thee as my boon
    companion
Not knowing Thy matchless greatness.
I have seen what was never seen before
At this I rejoice. But my heart is shaken with fear.
Show mercy, O God.[1]

And the special mercy he craves is an end to this insupport-
able vision. 'I ask to see Thee even as before' – not as
Absolute Brahman, but as Visnu, the gracious God who
has come to him as Krisna.[2]

Arjuna's request is granted. Krisna stands by his side as
before, the instruction continues as before, and this *Song of
the Lord* ends with the Lord communicating His 'highest
secret of all'.

What is this highest secret? Krisna referred to it thrice.
What is implied? That Brahman is to be conceived, in the
final analysis, as the impersonal absolute, 'the All', transcending all human definition? This may be the conclusion
if the intended reference is seen as a reference to the whole
text, with its central vision of Supreme Brahman and the
description of the several ways leading to union with
Brahman. It is a conclusion which may be encouraged by
the injunction to Arjuna, 'Act as thou thinkest best' (reflect
fully, use your intelligence) which follows the first mention
of the secret.[3]

But the second mention of the highest secret is followed
by a verse which has led others to conceive that the *Gita*'s
final word is on the side of a *bhakti* conception of Brahman,
identifying Supreme Brahman with a personal God in the
highest, a God who cares –

1. ibid., XI, 37 ff.   2. ibid., XI, 46.   3. ibid., XVIII, 65.

Worshipping Me, revering Me
So shalt thou come to Me:
I promise it, for thou art dear to Me.[1]

Christian teachers have held that God means the union of absolute power and absolute goodness. Is it something like this that the *Gita* is trying to say? Without this final word, 'Thou art dear to Me', Arjuna might just have been petrified by the power and glory of the great vision which brought him to his knees. But without the power and the glory of the vision, without the knowledge that Krisna signifies the majesty of the majestic, the assurance of this last word would not be the assurance needed for the way of *bhakti*.

Or does the *Gita* mean something very different and perhaps more subtle: that while there is no such reality as personal Brahman or personal God, the belief that there is such a reality may be psychologically or ethically helpful, for it spells the devotion which may take a man out of himself? Thence may follow the realization that there is no such small self to stand upon but only that greater reality which Brahman signifies. The first view may be called broadly theistic. The second view is often, though not very accurately, described as pantheistic.

Questions as to the *Gita*'s meaning arise because there are certainly passages in the *Gita* which encourage either view. It is tempting to engage in a discussion which has fascinated many commentators but it is sufficient for our present purpose to conclude that the *Gita* at least exhibits a tension between these two views, and to add that it is not an issue which may be decided by a mere comparison of different phrases and passages, noting for instance how much in the *Gita* comes straight from the Vedic scriptures. A modern approach to the study of religion with its regard for the more poetic expressions of faith and the manner of

1. ibid., XVIII, 63.

such expression means a greater regard for the fact, than might otherwise be the case, that the *Gita* tells a *story*. We are then to consider the intention behind this story. And how it may be fulfilled. If the intention of the *Gita* is to encourage bewildered man to go forward with that trust and confidence in God which is signified by the *bhakti* way of loving devotion, could this intention be fulfilled by a conclusion that God, when all is said and done, is just a pious fiction?

Our present purpose, however, takes us beyond the *Gita* itself to the wider context and larger history of the Hindu tradition. The *Gita* has simply served as the mirror of this tradition. The question posed in the *Gita*: Who or What is Brahman? is a central question in Hindu thought, a question which might also be put as: Who is God?

There are hints of this question in the very dawn of Vedic thought. 'Who knows for certain? Whence was it born and whence came this creation?'[1] By the end of the Vedic period the question has come to fuller expression and received fuller answer. It is pondered in many passages of the *Upanisads*, with reference to cosmic Brahman, for example, as that 'which holds the sun and moon to their duty, earth and heaven to their places ... seasons and years to their courses':[2] 'that which is below and is above, that which is to the west and to the east, that which is to the south and to the north ... indeed, the whole universe.'[3] The cosmos is likened to an 'eternal fig tree'. Its root is named Brahman –

> On it all the worlds do rest
> And no one ever sees beyond it.
> This, verily, is That![4]

1. *Rig Veda*, X, 129.
2. *Brihadaranyaka Upanisad*, III, viii. 9.
3. *Chandogya Upanisad*, XXV, 25.1; *Mundaka Upanisad*, II, ii. 11.
4. *Katha Upanisad*, VI, 1.

But even as Vedic man looks around him, faced by the riddle of the universe, he also looks within himself, confronted by the mystery of his own secret life. He comes to see his own smaller self in relation to a great self named the Atman. In fact, it might be said that such introspection is primary in Hindu thought. Anyone who has lived beneath India's warm sun and knows how the climate there so often tends to check the kind of vigorous physical activity which comes more naturally in colder northern climes will better understand how this may be so. They may also understand how the vigorous Aryans, as they come south, begin to think less of robust gods such as Indra and, sitting in meditation in some quiet forest glade, begin to ponder the significance of their own interior life. They ask what happens to a man when he dreams. They ask is life itself just a great dream. What does it mean to awake from the dream? What is the reality beneath the dream and the awakening?

> A certain wise man, while seeking immortality,
> Introspectively beheld the Self face to face. . . .

. . . .

> That whereby one perceives both
> The sleeping state and the waking state[1]

This train of thought ends in the equation, *tat tvam asi,* that thou art –

> Uddalaka, Son of Aruna told his son Svetaketu . . . This true Being, this subtle source of the world, that is the soul of everything that is Truth, that is the Self, THAT THOU ART, O Svetaketu.[2]

There follows what Hindu writers have named the 'happy' equation. The two lines of reflection converge in the conception of the Absolute, the Ultimate One as

1. *Katha Upanisad*, IV, 1 ff.   2. *Chandogya Upanisad*, VI, viii. 4–7.

Brahman–Atman. Thus far there is general agreement among these Vedic philosopher-seers.

But two positions arise with the question as to how much is known and how much can be said in the final analysis about this ultimate Primal Being. The general trend of thought in the *Upanisads* is monistic, with sharp distinction between the One ultimate reality – One without a second[1] – and the apparent Many-ness of the world and its inhabitants. In this context the classic statement, 'Brahman is all this', amounts to saying that the apparent plurality of 'all this' is deceptive. It follows that all attempts to define the One in terms of what we think we see and know around us, are misleading. In the long run of thought, none of the attributes by which we normally describe the phenomenal world can be ascribed to Absolute Brahman: Brahman is without attributes, *nirguna Brahman* – not this, not that (*neti, neti*).[2] There is, however, an implicit quali-fication. If the spirit in man can be identified with the great Self (Atman), and Atman can be equated with Brahman, it follows that Brahman is at least conceived as spiritual. At the same time, the 'not this, not that' guards against the idea that Absolute Brahman is merely small man writ large. Room may be left for a conception of Brahman as suprapersonal, but not for any purely anthro-pomorphic conception, and a good many passages in the *Upanisads* suggest such a suprapersonal conception. The Supreme Being, for example, is said to initiate and con-trol: 'He bethought Himself: let us now create worlds.'[3] He is 'the one controller who makes his one form manifold'.[4]

1. ibid., VI, ii. 1–3.
2. *Brihadaranyaka Upanisad*, II, iii. 6. The indication of this person (Brahman) is not this, not this . . . as to the name [of the Brahman] it is the truth beyond the truth.
3. *Aitareya Upanisad*, I, i. 1–3.   4. *Katha Upanisad*, V, 12.

These and similar statements having to do with Brahman's relation to the world suggest a Brahman with attributes, *saguna Brahman*, and indeed with personal attributes, a Brahman who might possibly be identified with the personal god, Isvara, of Hindu worship. In one passage, indeed, it is suggested that the world of beings has come to be because the Supreme One desired company.[1] In another passage we read –

> He encircled all things, radiant and bodiless, . . .
> All-seeing, all-wise, all-present, self-existent
> He has made all things well.[2]

There is, however, no developed systematic statement in these scriptures. All that can be said is that the scriptures provide grist for the mills of both theistic and monistic interpretations which come later in Hindu story, with more grist, perhaps, for the monist than for the theist.

The monistic interpretation is usually associated with the Vedantic philosophy subtly expounded by Sankara in the ninth century A.D. (the term Vedantist being used in this case with reference to a particular school of thought), while the theistic interpretation is similarly associated with Sankara's critic, Ramanuja, who lived in the thirteenth century A.D. Ramanuja is seen as providing a philosophic foundation for the *bhakti* piety which began its course long before Ramanuja's own day, a piety spread through India by fervent poets and singers such as the seventh-century Tamil mystic whose God 'filled [him] in every limb with love's mad longing'.[3]

Bhakti piety was more attuned to the poetic expressions of Hindu faith presented in the great epics and the *Purana*

1. *Brihadaranyaka Upanisad*, I, iv. 2.
2. *Isa Upanisad*, 8.
3. F. Kingsley and G. E. Phillips, *Hymns of the Tamil Saivite Saints*, Calcutta, 1921, pp. 121 ff.

stories naming the high gods Visnu and Siva than to the philosophical speculations of the *Upanisads*. But here again any attempt at brief summary or classification is misleading, for the *bhakti* movement went very much its own way. It was not confined to any one of the schools, monistic or theistic, nor to any one of the sects, Visnaivite nor Saivite, which developed through this same period, a period which began in the centuries preceding the Christian era and produced the Hinduism encountered by the British and other traders from the West in the eighteenth century: the Hinduism of the rival schoolmen, many of them followers of Sankara maintaining debate with the followers of Ramanuja; the Hinduism of the sects, worshippers of Visnu and worshippers of Siva, repeating the legends of Krisna or of Ram; the Hinduism of the castes, and of the *brahmin*'s prestige; the Hinduism of the *maths*, societies of the faithful acknowledging the guidance of some one particular teacher and his predecessors; the Hinduism of the temples and of local cults maintaining devotion to some particular god; the Hinduism of the thousands of villages maintaining practices and beliefs which began in India before the coming of the Aryans; the Hinduism of the household shrines to be found in every Hindu home (for Hinduism is indeed very much a family religion, maintained by family rituals), the Hinduism which turns to the *guru*, the inspired teacher, out of the same respect for vision which prompts regard for the holy scripture. All of this, and more, is Hinduism, and it is this Hinduism to which the way of *bhakti* belongs, bringing with it warmth and devotion and new scrutiny of all that tends to what is merely external or superficial.

As already noted, our revised modern understanding of Hindu faith is largely due to the fresh account which is now taken of the history and significance of this *bhakti* movement. It is a mistake, however, to separate the *bhakti* movement and name it, as did Rudolph Otto, *another* religion. It is indeed a religion of grace, but it should be seen as something which is very much at the heart of the total expression of Hindu faith.

It is also a mistake to associate *bhakti* theism too narrowly with Ramanuja's interpretation. There are followers of Sankara who would insist that there is as much room in Sankara's school as in any other for genuine devotion to God. Sankara's position, it is claimed, is indeed *advaita*, in opposition to dualism, but it is not rigorously monistic and certainly not pantheistic. The difficulty with Sankara's interpretation, from the standpoint of the theist, lies in his description of two levels of thought. At the one level man, subject to the deceptive power named *maya*, may ascribe the world to a personal god, Isvara – the living god-principle worshipped under such names as Visnu and Siva – but when he attains a higher level of vision, piercing through all that is illusory, he will know that the only reality is Brahman, *nirguna Brahman*, spaceless, timeless, eternal, not to be conceived in terms of time and space; not to be conceived in terms of *this* in space or time or *that* in space or time. Carried to an extreme this may be seen as leading to the kind of view presented by Dr Sarma when he observes that Hindus are taught

that the particular name and form of any deity are limitations which we in our weakness impose on the all-pervading Spirit, which is really nameless and formless. . . . Even the common people are taught that the worship of a personal god is only a half-way house in man's journey to the Ultimate Reality . . .

The Supreme Being is a person only in relation to ourselves and our needs . . . the highest theism is only a sort of glorified anthropomorphism, but we cannot do without it. The heart of man hungers for a god of love, grace, and mercy.[1]

1. D. S. Sarma, 'Nature and History of Hinduism' in *The Religion of the Hindus*, ed. Morgan, p. 11.

For the resolute theist this will not do, even allowing for Dr Sarma's careful qualifications. For such a theist it is not enough to say that Hinduism at its highest neither rejects theism nor accepts it, as does Dr Sarma. God can only be God if he is God in the highest, the most ultimate reality. At the same time, the *neti neti* of Hindu Absolutism may also be allowed by the theist. Even when Brahman is conceived as Personal God it may still be acknowledged that His Ultimate Reality transcends human thinking in much the same way as Christian theologians allow for the Hidden God and distinguish between divine revelation and human understanding of that revelation.

Here it may be noted that a good many Hindus today make use of the term revelation with reference to their own thought. Referring to the Vedic scriptures, for example, Dr Raghavan says that 'the various names by which they are known make clear that they are ancient knowledge, *revealed* to men'.[1] Whether the Hindu conception of Revelation is quite the same as the Christian (or the Muslim), is open to question and it is open to still further question when the discussion is sharpened by the Christian view that Revelation is centred in Christ as against the Hindu view of the avatar which implies that there may be many Christs. Here again, however, it is questionable whether any of the many 'Christs' of Hindu thought fulfil quite the same function as does the Christ of Christian thought in regard to Revelation. It is not generally held that Krisna in the *Gita* brought any 'new testament'. The *Gita* is rather valued as presenting what was already known through other sources.

To conclude that Hinduism presents a much more extensive and persistent body of theistic thought and faith than is sometimes supposed does not mean that what we

1. V. Raghavan, 'Introduction to the Hindu Scriptures', in *The Religion of the Hindus*, ed. Morgan, p. 265: italics mine.

have in the Hindu tradition is just a parallel to what may be found in western monotheistic religions. Nor is the theistic tradition to be ascribed merely to western influence. Of the older schools there is only one school which clearly reflects Christian influence and that is the school of Mahdva, who taught that salvation did not mean *union* with God; it meant drawing close to God, for God is eternally distinct from man and it is only by God's grace that man can attain such salvation. While some of the modern movements in India such as the Brahma Samaj may reflect western influence, they remain very distinctively Hindu. Nor is the theistic trend mainly sustained in India today by such movements. It is largely kept alive by the vigorous and organized activity of some of the Hindu *maths*, including the Lingayats of Mysore State and the Saiva Siddhanta *maths* of South India. Members of these *maths* write and distribute pamphlets and books furthering their views and they have established chairs in some of the universities.

Nor does the influence of western opinion necessarily mean the encouragement of theistic trends. Besides the scepticism which is growing apace in India today there is the influential philosophy of Sri Aurobindo as well as the interpretation of Hindu thought presented by India's great philosopher-statesman, Dr Radhakrishnan. Both of these indeed show the influence of western thought yet both exhibit monistic trends. The evangelists of the very active and resolute Ramakrishna Mission also maintain monistic standpoints.

It is the fact that Hinduism presents both of these standpoints, theistic and monistic, held together in fruitful tension in one and the same tradition, in one and the same stream of history, which gives Hindu thought its distinctive quality. The persistence of theistic trends brings Hinduism much more alongside Christian thought than has sometimes been realized. It means a Hinduism which amounts to something more than a flat challenge opposed to what is presented by the great monotheistic religions of the West. For many Hindus as for many Christians the central question is: what think ye of God? The fact that this question may be identified with the question: what think ye of Brahman? adds to the interest of Hindu thought from the standpoint of the philosopher of religion. Some of the positions maintained are indeed comparable with positions maintained in the West, but they are maintained in a different environment.

III

The Buddhist Tradition

IF it is appropriate to begin an introduction to the Hindu tradition with a story, the story told in the *Bhagavad Gita*, it is even more appropriate to begin with a story in the case of the Buddhist tradition. Indeed it might be argued that when it comes to Buddhism there is no choice in the matter, for the Buddhist tradition, unlike the Hindu, is one which begins with a particular founder at a particular time in human history. The story to be told is the story of this founder, Siddhattha Gotama the Buddha who lived, taught and died on the soil of northern India some five hundred years before the Christian era.

Some might object that a good part of this story is legendary and that all that a strict historian would allow might be written on the back of a postcard, amounting to no more than the bald statement that Gotama the Buddha lived several centuries before the Christian era, that he renounced his high estate and palace comforts as the son and heir of a rajah of the Sakyan clan in northwest India to become a wandering ascetic in search of higher truth (*dharma*); that the turning point of his career came when he turned from a fruitless asceticism to engage in a resolute meditation, attaining the special insight which meant that he was now called the Buddha or the Enlightened One; that he then taught an increasing number of followers the doctrine of the Middle Way with promise that if they followed this Way they themselves would attain a similar enlightenment; and that these same followers constituted the monastic order which he left at the end of a long life to preach and maintain his teaching.

All that has been added to this statement may be legendary, but legendary additions cannot be ignored if the devout Buddhist, 'the follower of the Buddha', is seen, as he very well may be seen, as one who seeks to be conformed to the likeness of the Buddha, having in mind not only his teaching but his character. For any understanding of the Buddhist faith, it follows that we must take into account the impression the Buddha made on his followers and the portrait of the Buddha as millions of Buddhists have seen that portrait throughout Buddhist history. What has been said of the story of another great religious founder, the Prophet Muhammad, can be said with equal truth of this story of the Buddha: we need

to become acquainted with the great personalities of the world religions dressed in those garments in which the pious faith of their followers have clothed them. The manger of Bethlehem and the song of the angels belong to the portrait of Jesus, and the fourfold contact with suffering and the renunciation of the pleasures of the palace to the portrait of Buddha. Something of the magic of their personalities, which we might not understand in any other way, speaks to us through the poetry of faith.[1]

We begin, then, with the legend of the Buddha.[2] One of the most significant chapters in the legend of the Buddha is that which relates his Great Renunciation and his Going Forth, with emphasis on what he has to renounce, together with equal emphasis on the hindrances placed in the way of his renunciation.

He is a prince, the son and heir of a king, a king descended from eighty-two thousand previous kings, ruling a city which is great, powerful and illustrious. In previous existences this young prince has resolved to become a

1. Tor Andrae, *Mohammed: The Man and His Faith*, New York, Harper Torchbook Edition, 1960.
2. There are various versions of this legend. I have followed the version given by Bishop Bigandet, *The Life or Legend of Gaudama: The Buddha of the Burmese*, first printed and published in Rangoon, Burma in 1858; third edition published in London, 1879.

Buddha and has grown in virtue. His present birth has been proclaimed by thirty-two mighty wonders. A lovely child, he grows up to firm manhood. He is very happily married and has a son. He is surrounded by every luxury, passing 'from one palace into another, moving as it were in a circle of ever-renewed pleasures and amusements'. Yet he proves that he is 'fully conversant with the eighteen sorts of arts and sciences'. He is clearly destined for greatness.

But there remains some doubt about the shape of this high destiny. It has been foretold that he will either become a mighty ruler bringing all nations under his sway, or a Buddha, 'the instrument for promoting the welfare and merits of all mortals'. When his father is told of this prediction, he is disturbed. He is a good man, beneficent and liberal, 'religiously observing the five precepts and the ten rules of kings', but he has no wish to see his son become a Buddha, which means becoming a hermit. He wants him to become a great monarch. Making inquiries, the king is told that his son will indeed become a hermit if he sees four signs: an old man, a sick man, a dead man, and a recluse. The king immediately does all in his power to prevent his son seeing these omens. Guards are placed 'in every direction at distances of a mile, charged with but one care, that of keeping out of his son's sight the appearance of these fatal omens'.

All precautions, however, are in vain. Driving in his carriage one day the young prince sees the first omen, an old man, the body bending forward with grey hairs, shrivelled skin, leaning upon a heavy staff, presenting 'the disgusting infirmities of old age'. Hearing this the king is alarmed. The guard is doubled. New enticements are devised. The king gives orders 'to bring to his son's palace the prettiest and most accomplished dancing girls, that in the midst of ever-renewed pleasure, he might lose sight of the thought of ever entering the profession of a hermit'.

But these devices fail. The son comes to see what the king does not want him to see: the signs which betoken the lot of humanity, old age, sickness, death. But he also sees the sign betokening emancipation, the sublime and dignified hermit, pointing 'the only way of life the wise man would wish to follow'.

There are vivid scenes depicting his growing disillusionment with the life of the palace and all sensual distractions. He wants to be free of it all and free of his own passions. More and more he becomes 'confirmed in his contempt for all worldly pleasures'. Even the birth of his son is seen as another tie which must be broken. He is ready to depart, ready for the Great Renunciation.

The hour comes for the dramatic Going Forth. It is night-time. With a last glance at his sleeping wife and son, he leaves the palace, mounts his horse, passes through the city gate and comes to a river. He spurs his horse and the fierce animal leaps at once to the opposite bank. There Gotama rids himself of his princely finery. He unsheathes his sword and 'seizing his comely hairs, cuts them with a single stroke'. He says a firm farewell to his servant, leaves his horse behind, and, donning the robes of a hermit, seeks the solitude of the forest.

His quest has begun. For six arduous years he wanders from place to place, meeting with other hermits, seeking instruction, 'unshaken in his purpose', joined for a time by five ascetics who are later to become his first followers. He practises extreme asceticism, fasting until he faints from utter weakness. At length he comes to the River Ganges and the Bodhi tree near Benares and begins the sustained Meditation which ends in the Great Enlightenment. In thus attaining the insight and bliss which is nirvana, he not only sees human life for what it is, beset by pain and misery, ignorance and vain craving, holding men in 'the vortex of existences'; he discerns the Four Noble Truths and the

THE STUDY OF RELIGIONS

Path which holds promise of emancipation. 'Whilst these thoughts passed through his mind, a little before the break of day ... the perfect science broke at once over him: he became the Buddha.'

Those who hear this story told, as thousands of devout Buddhists do today in Burma and other countries of south-east Asia, are left in no doubt as to its momentous consequences for themselves and for all sentient beings. The legend presents the Great Enlightenment as an event of cosmic interest. Demons and gods gather around, some of them hostile, some of them friendly. The whole wide universe is concerned –

When this great wonder took place, ten thousand worlds were shaken ... all the trees of ten thousand worlds shot out branches, loaded with fruits and flowers. The lilies bloomed ... the whole universe appeared like an immense garden covered with flowers: a vivid light illuminated the dark places ... rivers suspended their courses; the blind received their sight, the deaf could hear, the lame could walk. The captives were freed from their chains and restored to liberty.[1]

But what is there thus far in Gotama's life, it might be asked, to prompt such lyrical praise? What gospel is there here for the blind, the deaf, the lame, and the captives? If indeed the story ended here it could scarcely be presented as a clue to any poetry of faith. All that we have thus far is a portrait of Gotama, the Sage of the Sakyan clan, seeking wisdom with a resolution which is to be emulated. He may now indeed be called the Buddha, the Enlightened One. But what of that other title by which he is known, the title which suggests more of the warmth of religion: the Compassionate One? As yet there might seem little ground for it, but rather the contrary in this story of a prince who turns his back not only on the enticing luxuries of his high estate

1. Bigandet, op. cit., p. 97.

but also on his responsibilities, as prince, husband, and father.

But the legend does not end with the account of the Enlightenment. It proceeds to give account of a long, arduous ministry, pursued with a resolution as persistent as that which led to the Great Enlightenment itself, a ministry pursued for some forty-five years, a ministry which presents a Buddha who is not only the Sage, but indeed the Compassionate One. There are instances which particularly emphasize this compassion. It is told, for example, that, 'moved with compassion', the Buddha intervened to prevent a war between rival communities. The same 'compassionate heart' is said to have moved the Buddha to hurry to the deathbed of his father, relieve the father's pain and instruct him in the *dharma* so that the royal parent could die in peace.

At the end of his life, the Buddha is portrayed as showing a final solicitude for the members of the monastic Order he has gathered together during his ministry. He wants to make sure that they have really grasped his teaching. Devout Buddhists interpret this concern as a concern for all sentient beings, for it is through this Order, a missionary Order, that the teaching is to be spread throughout the world.

Thus the image of the Buddha presented in this legend is seen as the image of one whose character exhibits two principal virtues, wisdom and compassion. To know and accept the story is to see the Buddha not only as the great teacher but as the great example, and whatever else Buddhism may mean it must surely mean for those who treasure this story a resolution to be conformed to the same image and realize the same character.

Among Buddhists of the Theravada tradition in the countries of southeast Asia, it has indeed been a treasured story, told through the centuries, repeated again and again.

It is recalled to memory in many ways. A traveller in Burma, for example, even at the present day, may come upon a village where a young Burman is being prepared for his initiation. He may see the boy, dressed in princely attire, seated on a horse, riding in procession through the village. He may follow the boy back to his home where the monks and villagers have assembled for the initiation feast. He may see him dismount from his horse, leave his friends, enter the house and a few moments later return to the veranda, no longer dressed in princely attire, but wearing the yellow robe of a Buddhist novice. He may watch him depart with the monks, leaving his home for the weeks or months he may spend in the monastery to be instructed in the *dharma*. If the traveller knows this legend of the Buddha he will know very well what is in the boy's mind. He will understand that what has been taking place is a re-enactment of the great story. This boy is the prince Gotama, going forth from the palace, making the Great Renunciation. He is following in the Path. He is to be the Buddha's disciple. The traveller may also know that when the boy goes with the monks to live in the monastery and receive their instruction, the same high purpose may again be recalled as the boy recites the *Song of Eight Victories* recalling the Buddha's resistance against successive temptations and the virtues which enabled him to triumph:

> By patience and tranquillity
> (Such was his chosen panoply)
> The Sage achieved the victory
> Alavaka, the demon dread,
> The live long night he competed
>
> . . . .
>
> Be yours his glorious victory
> And yours its ample blessing be.

Nor can such a traveller fail to observe the many other

ways in which the Buddha's example will be recalled and brought home to this boy and others like him, in a country such as Burma where the Buddha is indeed a living memory, where 'the spire of his monastery marks every village', where the same familiar features of the same Gotama the Buddha are repeated in statue after statue. He will understand what the venerable scholar U Thittila means when he explains that while Buddhists do not, or should not, pray to the Buddha they may very well love to have before them the representation of some image of their Master which enables them to think of his virtues, his love and his compassion –

The words they recite are meditations and not prayers. They recite to themselves *the virtues of the Buddha*, his Dhamma, and his Holy Order so that they may acquire such mental dispositions as are favorable to the attainment of similar qualities in their own minds.[1]

This statement by one of the most scholarly monks in Burma today is the more significant because it occurs in a context in which there is strong emphasis on the Buddha's *teaching* as presented in the Theravada scripture, the *Pali Canon*. Together with the discipline there prescribed, it is this teaching which is called the medicine for sick humanity. Moreover, it is also emphasized that the Buddha expected his followers to probe the truth of this teaching for themselves in the light of reason. There was to be no *slavish* regard for the teacher. With all this emphasis on the teaching, however, U Thittila does not, as some western writers have done, separate the teaching from the life which lies behind it or ignore the devotion inspired by the remembrance of the Buddha himself, a neglect which is largely responsible for misleading presentations of

1. Maha Thera U Thittila, 'The Fundamental Principles of Theravada Buddhism', in *The Path of the Buddha*, ed. Kenneth Morgan, New York, 1956, p. 75. Italics mine.

Theravada Buddhism as a cold ethic without any religious undertones at all. Such presentations may indeed leave us wondering how a Buddhism of this kind could have held the allegiance of devoted believers for twenty-five hundred years or could have inspired the missionary zeal which carried the Buddha's teaching far beyond its Indian homeland. To conceive such a Buddhism, without any poetry of faith at the heart of it, is indeed to conceive a Buddhism which is foreign to history. In this respect there is reappraisal on the part of a good many western writers today, and need for it, as it is seen that the teaching and the story belong together.

A hint of this close association is contained in the credo known as the Three Jewels or (significantly) the Triple Gem:

> I go for refuge to the Buddha
> I go for refuge to the Dhamma (the Teaching)
> I go for refuge to the Sangha (the Monastic Order).

Again, significantly, it is written in the scriptures: 'Who sees Dhamma sees me (Buddha); who sees me, sees Dhamma.'

To observe this close association between the reference to the Buddha himself and the reference to his teaching is perhaps to remove some of the difficulties which stand in the way of western understanding of the teaching. There may be further understanding if we also look more closely at some of the central terms of this teaching and question some generally accepted English translations and interpretations. It is certainly difficult otherwise to find points of meeting between this teaching and western thought, especially Christian thought.

Buddhist teaching has for its starting point the diagnosis of the human situation and the remedy announced in 'the Four Noble Truths' which must be read against the background of a world view which is very different from that which is generally held in the West. As in the case of Hindu India, Buddhism sees this present span of human existence in terms of migration from one life to another and hence in terms of a long pilgrimage through the centuries and through the many worlds constituting a vast universe. It is in this setting that we also have the basic doctrine of Dependent Origination (Pali, *Paticcasamuppada*; Sanskrit, *Pratityasamutpada*), or the doctrine of the fundamental order of the universe which means that one thing follows from another and leads to another in causal sequence. Hence all is change and in process of change. Turn where we will, nothing in present existence is permanent. The Wheel of Life revolves, with sentient beings passing from one existence to another, be it as men or as gods or animals, be it on this earth or elsewhere, in the migratory *samsara* process. Nor is this by chance. What is reaped is what has been sown. What has been enacted in some distant past affects what is possible in the present, according to the law of *karma*.

The Four Noble Truths begin with the observation that existence involves *dukkha*. *Dukkha* is usually translated in English as 'suffering'. But it is doubtful whether this translation conveys at all adequately what the Buddhist has in mind. *Dukkha* is generally conceived as amounting to something less than sheer misery, agony, or distress and something more than pain or sorrow.[1] The term signifies the mental and physical ill which is observed to accompany sentient existence as we know it here and now in contrast to the unspeakable bliss of nirvana:

> ... Man this heavy load does bear. ...
> The laying down thereof is bliss.[2]

1. *Pali-English Dictionary*, Pali Text Society Edition, Luzac, 1959, p. 324.
2. H. C. Warren, *Buddhism in Translations*, Harvard, 1909, p. 60.

To attempt a more precise definition might be misleading rather than helpful. Here, indeed, we have a case in which the poetry of legend may be more illuminating than the prose of systematic doctrine and we may get a better understanding of what *dukkha* means to the Buddhist if we go back to the story, stand alongside the young prince Gotama and hear him exclaim, shocked and disturbed – even 'terrified' – at his first sight of shrivelled, feeble old age: 'Birth is indeed a great evil, ushering all beings into such a wretched condition!'

The Second Noble Truth, which continues the diagnosis, reflects the doctrine of Dependent Origination. It relates the experience of *dukkha* to an attachment to present existence (*samsara*) despite its load of ill, an attachment which amounts to sheer thirst or craving (*tanha*) which on Buddhist principles must be regarded as utterly foolish since it means attachment to what is impermanent. At the heart of this attachment there is a self-regard which must also be rejected as vain and deluded since anything which can be called the self is also impermanent, subject to change and decay.

No aspect of Buddhist thought is more puzzling to the western mind than the view of human nature which is here taken, although Buddhist apologists today are swift to say that they find much in modern western psychology which supports their view, a view crystallized in the *an-atta* (no self) doctrine. Instead of any human 'soul' or self, the doctrine postulates a coming together of five fleeting aggregates (*skandhas*) to constitute sentient being, five aggregates or 'streams' of (1) corporeal sensation (2) feeling (3) perception (4) mental conception and (5) consciousness. The negative thrust of this doctrine is evident enough, and it is emphasized by the popular illustration of the chariot. What is there here it is asked except a putting together of wheels, axles, chariot body, banner staff, yoke, reins, and goading stick? To what else can one point as constituting the chariot? Very well, then: to what else can one point than streams of sensation, feeling, etc., as constituting human nature? The ethical implications of the doctrine are also clear enough as they cut the ground away from any anti-social self-centredness by removing any self and insisting that human beings are no exception to the rule that 'all is change', all within man no less than all around him, nothing here to warrant his arrogance or greed.

But the doctrine raises a good many issues and leaves us asking questions when we come to the third and fourth noble truths which have to do with a remedy for human ill which depends upon a resolution, as firm as the Buddha's resolution, to be done with all vain craving and false attachment to all that is merely temporary and accept and practise an eightfold discipline, moral and mental, which is the Path to nirvana. For the follower of the resolute Buddha is here bidden to be similarly resolute. He is 'to swelter at the task'. Critics of the *an-atta* doctrine ask who, on this analysis, is there left to swelter. Whence this resolution? The answer sometimes given is that the *an-atta* doctrine does not amount to a denial of human personality; it is simply a denial of 'soul-theory'.

Questions in regard to this doctrine, however, persist. They are prompted again by the promise of the bliss of nirvana which concludes the statement of the Four Noble Truths. As already observed the view that nirvana means the end of life itself, annihilation, a view which has been prevalent in the West, has been challenged. It has been challenged by Buddhists themselves. What is extinguished is not life itself but the craving and vain attachments which indeed must be destroyed if nirvana, the goal of Buddhist aspiration, is to be attained.

Discussion of this subject, it may be noted, may be stimulated by the contemporary interest in religious language and informed by studies in Comparative Religion, for the Buddhist affirmation of nirvana is paradoxical and, as such, invites comparison with the affirmation of ultimate religious terms in other traditions. Over against the negative terms there are positive descriptive terms. Nirvana is described as the further shore, the harbour of refuge, the cool cave, the matchless island, the holy city. It is sheer bliss. But what is there in man to enjoy this bliss? The *an-atta* doctrine with its denial of soul theory appears to forbid comparison with doctrines of immortality found elsewhere, though not perhaps with some other interpretations of eternal life which are not so wedded to the conception of an imperishable, inherently immortal soul. Further questions arise as a distinction is drawn between the nirvana experience of the Buddha with his attainment of enlightenment in middle life and his passage to final nirvana (*parinibbana*) forty years later at the end of his long ministry. What became of the Buddha then? What, in final analysis, is our human destiny according to this Theravada Buddhist teaching? We are left it would seem with a clear statement about the Path to nirvana and the resolute effort required to attain this goal but with anything but a clear statement regarding the goal itself which nevertheless inspires this effort.

Indeed, in regard to this question of ultimate human destiny, as also in regard to all other questions of this kind, we have the agnosticism which is one of the most challenging features of Theravada Buddhism. In contrast to most other religious traditions, we have here, it might seem, not only a complete absence of any belief in God, or any approach to such a belief, but a complete absence of any experience or religious consciousness of transcendent Being. To those who believe in a God who has approached man everywhere and aroused in every human being some response to His presence, Theravada Buddhism presents a serious problem. In a recent attempt to deal with this issue, it has been plausibly argued that if we put together the four terms Dharma – Karma – Nirvana – Buddha which, for the Theravada Buddhist 'embraces the highest order of realities', and see these terms as constituting a 'deity-complex', we have some answer to this problem, not indeed an answer which amounts to an explicit belief in God comparable with Christian belief but an answer which betokens something comparable with religious response as Christians and others conceive it.[1]

There is, however, no avoiding the fact that the Buddha himself is presented as encouraging the agnosticism which his Theravada followers maintain. While they hesitate to describe the Buddha himself as an agnostic, since they would not question his full enlightenment,[2] they emphasize his dismissal of metaphysical speculations as pertaining only 'to the jungle, the desert, the puppet show, the writhing, the entanglement of speculation . . . conducing neither to wisdom nor to insight'.

Along with the absence of any belief in a divine being in this Theravada tradition, there is the absence of belief in divine grace, as man is bidden to work out his own salvation, dependent on his own effort. The nearest hint of any thought of divine grace is that which may be seen in the popular devotion to the Buddha himself, the constant recalling of his virtue, the gratitude for the enlightenment which enabled and prompted him to make known the Path to nirvana, and the persuasion that, by token of this enlightenment, there is none other to be compared with him. But some may see in all this devotion a very large hint indeed and one that prepares us for the revised version of

1. cf. Winston L. King, *Buddhism and Christianity*, Philadelphia, 1962, pp. 34, ff.
2. cf. K. N. Jayatilleke, *Early Buddhist Theory of Knowledge*, London, 1963, pp. 470 ff.

the Buddhist faith to be found in the Mahayana tradition, where the Buddha is revered as the glorified eternal Buddha and, in a parable which invites comparison with the Christian parable of the prodigal son, presented as the Father of all sentient beings, not only instructing them but assisting them in the Path by the grace of his abiding presence and solicitude.

The scripture containing this parable, *The Lotus of the Wonderful Law*, provides us with a good introduction to Mahayana Buddhism, although it is only one of many scriptures, variously estimated and not all of them read or known in this Mahayana tradition which, in its diversity, stands in sharp contrast to the Theravada tradition where the sole and sufficient reference is to the scripture constituting the *Pali Canon*, written in Ceylon some centuries after the Buddha's death.

One explanation of the rich diversity of thought and practice presented in the Mahayana tradition is the fact that the Mahayana interpretation, developed in India in the first centuries of the Christian era was further developed in China and Japan where it did not have the field to itself but was subject to Confucian, Taoist, and other influences. Another explanation is that the Mahayana teachers were from the first more prone to speculation than their Theravada brethren.

The *Lotus* scripture, however, attributes the Mahayana version to the Buddha himself.

Written in the first or second century A.D., with some chapters probably added at a later date, the *Lotus* scripture is a dramatic announcement of the Mahayana gospel. While it is presented as a development of the Buddha's teaching, announced by the historic Buddha himself at the end of his ministry, there is no question about it being, so to speak, a *new* testament. It amounts to a revised version of the Buddha's farewell. Instead of a farewell which leaves his followers with no more than a teaching which shows them the Path, leaving unanswered questions as to what happens to the Buddha now that he has come to final nirvana, as in the Theravada account, we have a version in which the Buddha is saying in effect: 'Lo I am with you always.' He is with his followers always because he is the abiding, eternal Buddha.

The announcement takes the form of a cosmic drama, with a stage set against the background of eternity. Expectation is aroused from the beginning as the reader is introduced to a vast, excited assembly including Buddha beings from all the quarters of the whole wide universe –

Thus have I heard. Once upon a time the Lord was staying at Ragagriha on the Vulture Mountain with a numerous company of noble saints, monks of the order ... eighty thousand Bodhisattvas ... sixty thousand gods. ... Thus it was that the Lord, surrounded, attended, honoured, revered, venerated, worshipped ... sat cross-legged on the seat of the law and entered upon the meditation termed 'the station of the exposition of Infinity', his body motionless, his mind perfectly tranquil. ... And there fell a great rain of divine flowers ... while the whole Buddha field shook in six ways ... trembling from one end to the other ... and all gazed on the Lord in astonishment, in amazement, in ecstasy. ... And there issued a ray from between the eyes of the Lord ... extending over eighteen hundred thousand Buddha fields. ...

Then arose in the mind of Bodhisattva Mahasattva Maitreya the thought: O how great a wonder does the Tathagata display! What may be the cause, what the reason?[1]

The reason appears as the drama proceeds, with scenes of increasing wonder and mounting tension on the part of an audience which increases in size, with more and more Buddha beings crowding the vast stage. There is a climactic

1. tr. from W. E. Soothill, *The Lotus of the Wonderful Law*, Oxford, 1930.

moment, when a great tower arises from the earth reaching high into the heavens. In the tower there is a throne and a voice from the throne is heard –

Excellent, excellent, Lord Sakyamuni! Thou hast well expounded the *Dharma* of the Lotus of the Wonderful Law.

and the Buddha is seen to ascend from the earth and share this throne with the ancient Buddha who has thus spoken. What is thus approved as excellent is a statement by the Buddha that the teaching given throughout his ministry is good as far as it goes but it does not go far enough. It has pointed the Path which has to be followed in order to attain nirvana. But this teaching needs to be completed by the assurance that all sentient beings can and will attain this goal by the further help that they may now expect from the Buddha, and assurance comes when they realize from whence the first teaching has come. It has come, not just from the Buddha as they have hitherto conceived him, but from Buddha who is now made more fully known to them: the eternal Buddha with resources and power beyond any that they may have imagined; the Buddha whose wisdom means an understanding of the condition and capacities of each and every sentient being; whose compassion is such that by all appropriate and tactful means he is constantly seeking to come to their aid, to awaken them to the marvellous potentialities of their own inherent Buddha nature. Moreover, the Buddha who thus speaks is not alone. In attendance upon him now are many, many Buddha beings from all the quarters of the universe, many, many Bodhisattvas engaged in the great continuous ministry for the salvation of all sentient beings, delaying their own final nirvana attainment for this high purpose. All this is told in scene after scene of cosmic wonder, with one image crowding upon another to enlarge the marvel of it all.

Whatever else the devout reader may conclude from

these pages he must surely conclude that his life is surrounded and embraced by the Buddha power. Far from being left entirely to his own poor devices he is encompassed on every side by a Buddha power which invites his trust, awakens his faith and inspires his resolution.

To bring this conclusion home, the curtain descends at intervals and what is thus told in breath-taking drama is also told in simple parable. One of these parables depicts the Buddha as a wise father whose prodigal son returns home not realizing at first that he has indeed come home, not recognizing his father after the long lapse of years, a prodigal in such vile, debased, and menial condition that the father sees that he cannot immediately hail him as his son and heir but must first restore him to his true manhood and dignity. The moral is drawn that all men everywhere, indeed, all sentient beings, are the Buddha's sons, objects of his unceasing, effective concern, 'though we had no mind to hope or expect it'.

The name, *Mahayana*, signifies that larger understanding of the Buddha's path which is claimed in this scripture. It means the great (*Maha*) vehicle (*yana*), the term, vehicle, reflecting the conception of Buddhist doctrine as a raft which carries sentient beings across the ocean of present existence to the opposite shore of nirvana. In contrast, Theravada teaching is named *Hinayana*, signifying an inadequate understanding on the part of those who reject Mahayana views, foolishly contented, it is said, with 'but a trifle of nirvana'. Theravada Buddhists naturally object to this description. They prefer the name Theravada, which signifies their allegiance to the Buddhist teaching as transmitted by elders (*theras*) regarded as orthodox.

While there was some anticipation of Mahayana doctrine before the first centuries of the Christian era, it was during this period that the practices and teachings which may broadly be described as Mahayana came more and more into view. It is sometimes said that in India itself Mahayana Buddhism took the place of Theravada Buddhism, which is described as having everything for the monks and nothing for the laity. As late as the eighth century A.D., however, Mahayana and Hinayana monks were found living together in the same monasteries. They observed the same monastic discipline: 'Those who worship the Bodhisattvas and who read the Mahayana *sutras* get the name of Mahayanists; those who do not are Hinayanists.'[1] There was, indeed, much in this Mahayana development which made swift appeal to imagination, much to enlist new popular interest, much to make it a Buddhism for the laity. It was a missionary Buddhism, with fervent evangelists on mountain paths and strange highways which would bring them to central Asia and to China. The new appeal to the masses coincided with new forms of Buddhist art which appeared in the northwestern empire of King Kanishka in the second century A.D. in response to Greek and Persian influences. From now on there were the Buddha images and monuments which were to become so closely associated with popular devotion throughout the Buddhist world. There was also a growing Buddhist mythology. There was poetry. The ballads of the *Lalitavistara* (*The History of the Play of the Buddha*) which was the basis of Sir Edwin Arnold's *The Light of Asia* became the poetry of Asvaghosha's *Buddhacarita* (*The Course of the Buddha*), with its announcement of the Enlightened One as

a lotus, unsoiled by passion, sprung from the lake of knowledge; a cloud bearing the water of patience, pouring forth the ambrosia of the good Law ... causing all the shoots of healing to grow; a sun that destroys the darkness of delusion[2]

1. I-Tsing (*c*.700) quoted by Edward Conze, *Buddhism: Its Essence and Development*, p. 122.

2. *Sacred Books of the East*, Vol. XLIX: *The Buddha Karita of Asvaghosha*, trans. by E. B. Cowell, Oxford, 1894, Bk. XIV, 82–85, p. 157.

Along with this Buddhism for the masses there was a Buddhism for the philosophers. There was new intellectual vitality, stimulated by the similar vitality of revived Brahmin challenge. It was a day of great dialogue. Buddhist logicians at Nalanda continued a lively debate with Brahmin logicians at Mithila across the River Ganges for some seven hundred years. Two great schools of Buddhist thought were established. First there was the Madyamika doctrine, expounded by Nagarjuna. In our own day this has been named the central philosophy of Buddhism by the Hindu scholar, T. R. V. Murti – central because it may be seen to follow from the Theravada negations while at the same time preparing the way for the idealistic affirmations of the second great Mahayana school, the Yogacara (or the Vijnanavada) which was expounded by the brothers, Asanga and Vasubandhu in the fourth century A.D. The Madyamika school might be described as proposing a middle way between Hindu affirmation of the *Atman* (the Great Self) and Theravada agnosticism on the subject:

That 'everything is permanent' is one extreme; that 'everything is transitory' is another . . . that '*ātman* is' (*ādmiti*) is one end (*antab*): that the '*atma* is not' is another . . . but the middle between the *atma* and *nairatmya* views is the Inexpressible.[1]

The wind of Mahayana doctrine was moving more in the direction of that Hindu absolutism which ended in the conception of ultimate reality as Brahman-Atman, setting the goal of life as union with Brahman. Nagarjuna and his followers also discerned an ultimate reality as they held that the Buddha had penetrated behind the changes and chances of this fleeting life and the goal they named was similarly positive: nirvana. Where they stopped short of Hindu absolutism was in their refusal to accept any *con-*

1. *Kasyaparivarta*, pp. 86–7, quoted by T. R. V. Murti, *The Central Philosophy of Buddhism*, London, 1955, p. 27.

ceptions of this ultimate reality whether in terms of Brahman, Atman, or in any other terms. On the contrary, they taught that such conceptions and all related theories should be avoided as the very things which might hinder the realization of ultimate reality. Their teaching was 'the antidote for all theories ... all dogmatic views ...'[1]. On this point they might have added that they remained staunch Buddhists, however near they might come to Hindu absolutism. They were still in the Path, for they were maintaining and emphasizing the Buddha's refusal to speak about reality in terms which could only lead to a confusion between reality and unreality. Professor Murti aptly calls their teaching the systematic form of the Buddha's silence.[2]

As far as language went they were even more resolute about this silence than the Theravadans. Whereas the Theravada interpretation was paradoxical, poised between positive and negative terms, the Madyamika philosophers preferred entirely negative terms. But the intention of these terms is fully and vigorously affirmative. The Buddha's silence is, to use a later phrase, a roaring silence. The same pressed lips which refused to name *conceptions* of nirvana are seen to affirm the *reality* of nirvana. Here again comparative studies are helpful. As in the case of paradoxical language, we find in other religious traditions a similar use of negative language to affirm an ultimate reality which is beyond the reach of our logic.

It is more important to make this affirmative intention clear because English translation of one of the basic terms of this doctrine often proves misleading. The Sanskrit term *sunyata* is translated void or emptiness, a translation which suggests sheer nihilism. Misunderstanding again may arise from the fact that in Buddhist art the void is

1. Quoted T. R. V. Murti, op. cit., p. 164.
2. T. R. V. Murti, op. cit., p. 35.

frequently represented by a stark circle which for most readers in the West just means zero; nothing; nothing at all. What this void within the circle may mean to a Buddhist, however, is indicated by Professor Nakamura when he writes: 'It is a living void, because all forms come out of it, and whoever realizes the void is filled with life and power and the bodhisattva's love of all beings.'[1]

The idealism of the Vijnanavada school which followed upon the heels of the Madyamika school posited different levels of consciousness until 'the consciousness that holds all' is attained and, thereby, nirvana. The thought here invites comparison with Hindu Vedanta conceptions of identification of the human soul with the indwelling Atman (the great Self which is All). There is ground, then, for the view that we have here in these early Mahayana schools a Buddhism returning home before it sets out again on that further missionary course which is to bring it to China and Japan.

Yet it remains 'the rebellious stepchild' holding to premises which are distinctively Buddhist and engaging in new discussions which have to do with these premises. Among such discussions is one dealing with the fundamental belief in causality or dependent origination. The emphasis in Theravada Buddhism is on temporal causal sequence with such sequences in the plural running through time, so to speak, side by side. The Mahayana teachers thought of causality in what may be called more horizontal terms, looking not so much to past or future as across the board. They taught the dependence of things on each other. Nothing exists of itself or by itself. There are no separate entities. This view of the relativity of all things had far-reaching implications, ethical and religious. It prompted an interpretation of the *an-atta* doctrine which

1. Hajime Nakamura, 'Unity and Diversity in Buddhism' in *The Path of the Buddha*, ed. Morgan, p. 381.

meant still further rejection of all notions of 'mine and thine'. The saint or *arhat* who might seem to be narrowly intent on his own salvation was taken from his pedestal and replaced by the *bodhisattva* full of realistic concern for others.

The expansion of Buddhism beyond the Himalayan ranges brought further diversity as it brought further dialogue, dialogue this time not with the parent faith but with such foreign traditions as Taoism, Confucianism, and Shintoism. The progress of Buddhism in China and Japan was amazing but Buddhism never took full possession in either of these countries. It remained one faith alongside others. It was a new and challenging environment which meant new schools and new masters. Even today some of the so-called new religions of Japan might be described as virtually revised schools of Buddhist interpretation.

In view of all this diversity, our account at this point can only be highly selective if it is to be something more than a catalogue of names. Brief references to two major variants, Zen and Pure Land Buddhism, may, however, be illuminating for here we have within one and the same tradition, two very different answers to a question which is fundamental in all religions: What must I do to be saved? Or, more especially: How much depends on my own efforts? Theravada Buddhists, as we have seen, answered that everything depends on one's own efforts. 'Monks, work out your own salvation.' That was one of the Buddha's last words. Zen Buddhists may be seen as maintaining this same answer. What is advocated is concentrated contemplation or *dhyana*, a Sanskrit term translated as *Ch'an* in China where Zen teaching originated in the sixth century A.D. It is a contemplation demanding that rigorous self-discipline and resolution which has been made familiar to the west by pictures of Zen novices sitting rigidly in rows on the four sides of a meditation hall. By such resolution they hope to realize *satori* (the nirvana enlightenment).

'Zen in its earnestness' writes Chisan Koho, 'is closer to Theravada Buddhism . . . than any other sect of Mahayana Buddhism.'[1] Zen is also closer to Theravada Buddhism in its regard for Gotama, the historical Buddha, who is said by the same writer to be 'the main object of adoration',[2] 'neither a Buddha conjured up in the imagination, nor an idealized Buddha devoid of real personality, but an actual historical personage.'[3] Dealing with the history of his own Soto Zen sect, he traces what might be named an apostolic succession back through the successive Zen patriarchs to the founder of Buddhism. He makes the significant remark that 'the successive patriarchs all live in the character of the Buddha' –

It is therefore said, your (obvious) face is not your real one. The real one is transmitted from the Buddha. When the false self dies within us, we find our life in that of the Buddha . . . in this way the life of the Buddha continues throughout history.[4]

Chisan Koho expressly adds that even when there is reference to the Mahayana doctrine of the triple body of the Buddha – the Eternal One; the Blessed One; and the Manifest One – this means no forgetting of the historical Gotama; 'the historical Buddha . . . unites (these) three aspects in his own person'.

But what, it may be asked, of the Zen master who is said to have turned to a young novice who sat piously and humbly before him, as stolid as a statue, shouting 'Get out of here. We have got enough stone Buddhas around in this monastery. We don't want any more.' The Zen Buddhist points out that there is here no disrespect of the Buddha himself. On the contrary, it is out of very respect for the

1. Chisan Koho, *Soto Zen*, Tokyo, p. 44.
2. ibid., pp. 75–6.   3. ibid., p. 61.
4. ibid., p. 71.

Buddha that the master cries out against such an apparently superficial and lifeless imitation, not of the Buddha's life but of the Buddha's statue.

'The uninterrupted transmission of the True Life starting from the Buddha is what we call ... "correctly transmitted Buddhism".'[1] To ensure this transmission written scripture is not enough. As water is poured from one vessel to another so the Word has to be passed from a living master to a living pupil. 'If one has a real desire to enter Buddhism', wrote the great teacher, Dogen, 'then one must not hesitate to go to a master for training even if it means ... crossing the seas and climbing mountains.' When it comes to what they have to say about *satori* (enlightenment) and what they regard as standing in the way of *satori*, Zen Buddhists are firmly in the Mahayana tradition. If the earlier Madyamika teaching can be described as 'the antidote of all theories', the shock treatment of slaps and blows, physical as well as mental, which to a good many western observers is the most distinctive feature of Zen, might be described as a sledge-hammer assault on all such theory. The essentials of Zen are frequently summarized in *The Four Statements*:

1. A special transmission *outside* the scripture.
2. No dependence on words or letters.
3. Direct pointing to the Mind of Man.
4. Seeing into one's own nature and the attainment of Buddhahood.

In rejecting dependence on words or letters, Zen masters set even firmer limits to human logic than do the Theravada or Madyamika teachers. The shock treatment is meant to enable the inquirer to realize these limits. As to the experience of *satori*, Zen masters differ from Theravada teachers in positing an enlightenment or intuitive grasp of truth not

1. ibid., p. 77.

only at the end of the Path, but here and now, as they persevere in the Path itself –

Soto sect *zazen* (meditation) is not a way leading to enlightenment, but a religious practice carried on in the state of enlightenment. This *zazen* differs from the meditation practised by the
Buddha before his enlightenment . . . it corresponds rather to
. . . the meditation . . . practised after the enlightenment of the
Buddha.[1]

The doctrine here goes far beyond anything Therava-
dists might say. It amounts to more than a claim to be a
follower of the Buddha. It surely means that in a sense the
Zen Buddhist sees himself as already Buddha or a Buddha-
being. In the Soto Zen sect, the great master Dogen is
quoted as taking the scriptural statement: 'All beings have
the Buddha nature' and construing it to mean 'All beings
are the Buddha nature'. He goes further: 'The Buddha
nature is everything'.[2]

What we have in Zen, it may be thought, is mystical
pantheism. Dr Suzuki grants the mysticism but he denies
the pantheism. He does so in a book which compares the
Zen conception of the Void with the conception of the
Christian mystic, Meister Eckhardt. Eckhardt also writes
of his void: 'The Godhead is as void as if it were not.'[3] But
it may also be noted that Eckhardt uses terms which recall
a quotation from the Taoist literature. Besides describing
the Godhead as a void he describes it as a well-spring.[4] Ru-
dolf Otto, when he compares Eckhardt's work with Indian
mysticism, ends by saying that Eckhardt had a mystical
experience which was also an experience of grace.[5] Accord-

1. ibid., p. 67.
2. ibid., p. 66.
3. R. Otto, *Mysticism East and West*, New York, Meridian Book
edition, 1957, p. 183.
4. D. T. Suzuki, *Mysticism: Christian and Buddhist*, p. 16.
5. Otto, op. cit., p. 201.

ing to Suzuki there is nothing like this in Zen Buddhism. Indeed, he says that it is the unique feature of Zen that whatever is accomplished is accomplished without resorting to such religious conceptions as God or grace.

The issues raised by Zen are not unknown to the West. They are familiar to all students of mysticism and they have been discussed by philosophers through the centuries. Nor are the issues raised narrowly related to the religious interest alone. They have to do with the broad question of the avenues of truth. Entering the western scene at a time when there are a good many second thoughts about the answers given by logical positivists and others, Zen gives sharper edge to some of the questions which have been raised while it invites consideration of new prospects and perhaps offers some new insights. The fundamental issue is the relation of intuition to logical reasoning. Granted the intuitive grasp of truth which the *satori* experience signifies, granted that it goes beyond the limits of our logic, what is its relation to such logic? Is it quite so opposite as the Zen analysis may suggest? Whereas Theravada exercises invite a sharpening of our wits the Zen *koans* invite despair of our wits before there can be any *satori*. Perhaps the fault, even on the Zen analysis, is not so much in our logic as in the uses to which it may be put. When Dr Suzuki observes that 'the worst enemy of Zen . . . is the intellect', he inserts the significant qualification 'at least in the beginning'.[1]

Pure Land Buddhism presents a very different outlook, especially when we turn to the Shinshu teaching which is the version of Buddhism most widely accepted in Japan today. Here indeed a Theravada Buddhist might wonder if he is still among cousins in the faith, let alone brothers in

1. Q. W. Barrett, *Zen Buddhism: Selected Writings of D. T. Suzuki*, New York, 1956, p. 147.

the faith. What could he make of the piety expressed in the hymn –

> Have ye faith in Amita's Vow
> Which takes us in eternally.
> Because of Him, of his Great Grace
> The Light Superb will all be thine.[1]

Amita's Vow? What is this? A Buddha (Amita) who has taken the place of Gotama, the historic Buddha, an Amita who has made some kind of vow which leads so-called Buddhists to depend upon 'his Great Grace' instead of relying upon their own resolute efforts? Zen with its notions of *satori* and enlightenment before the journey's end was difficult enough to accept as Buddhism, such an observer might exclaim, but this Pure Land abandonment of the very idea of working out one's own salvation, without resort to any other power, how can this be Buddhism?

A scripture of special significance for Pure Land Buddhism is the *Great Sutra of the Endless Life (Sukhavativyuha Sutra)*. Gotama the Buddha is again making an announcement from the Vulture Mountain. His subject this time is the virtue of Amitayus, the Buddha of Infinite Life, and the wonders of the western paradise which he has established where there is 'no withering and no change'. The light that issues from the person of this Buddha, says Gotama, outshines all others. 'None of the lights of all other Buddhas can equal it. It shines upon a hundred Buddha countries or a thousand Buddha countries': it is boundless, unhindered, burning light, pure light, joy-breeding light, incessant light, inexpressible light. Hence it is that this Amitayus Buddha is also named Amitabha, and the two names are combined in the Japanese term Amita.

1. *The Shinshu Seiten: the Holy Scriptures of Shinzu*, The Honpa Hongwanji Mission of Hawaii, 1955, p. 236.

In this same scripture it is told how this Amita Buddha was formerly the mendicant monk, Dharmakara, who was so full of solicitude for others that he only wanted the highest blessedness if he could share it with others. He made a number of vows expressing this purpose. His eighteenth vow affirmed that all who sincerely trusted in him and 'thought accordingly' would indeed come to the Pure Buddha realm which he would establish.

What it means to 'think accordingly' has been variously interpreted by the different Pure Land Schools. It is agreed that it means to have trust and faith in Amita but how is this trust expressed and sustained? 'What more, if anything, is required than the recital of his name' – the *Nembutsu* (*Namu Amita Butsu*)?

The scripture promises that all who have this faith in Amita and trust in the 'power of his vows' will, at the hour of their death, find Amita Buddha at their side waiting to conduct them to his western paradise, 'ten billion countries away from here'. In scripture and in Pure Land poetry this paradise is described in terms which recall the Christian description of the heavenly Jerusalem. There are 'trees of gold, silver, lapis lazuli, crystal and coral; and delicate symphonies'; bathing ponds of pure, clean, and fragrant water, with sands of gold, silver, amber, or white chalcedony, bordered by groves of sandalwood trees. But as if to ward off any interpretation that what is here presented is merely sensual delight, the scripture adds that while rich banquets may be spread none partake of them. For 'the body and mind soften and the taste clings not ... that Buddha's country is pure and peaceful ... It is like the Uncreate and is like Nirvana itself'. In brief, what this pure realm provides for the pilgrim on the Path is a new spiritual environment, far different from what he has known on earth. Here, surrounded by others of radiant faith, here in the presence of Amita and other Buddha beings, here where the only voices heard are true and noble – 'the voice of the Law, the voice of the Brotherhood, the voice of Nirvana ... the voice of the Great Compassion' – here there will be no falling back. It is the rightly established 'unretrogressive state' –

> Now the soul is set free from the haunts of darkness
> And rests secure in the dwelling of truth.
> See, all that was dim and beclouded on earth
> Here is revealed, appropriated, secured.[1]

It is the promise of the Great Physician moved by pity for a sick and impure world.[2] And man is seen in desperate need of this relief. Together with this Buddhist doctrine of grace there is what might be described as a doctrine of original sin –

> No true heart find I e'er in me
> It is hard to check our evil thoughts
> The mind like asps and scorpions runs. ...
> Deeds righteous are mixed with poison
> If His Grace were not, how could I
> Cross the sea, where e'er life's storms rave. ...
> The age is vile ... corrupt and all-vile.[3]

The popular parable ascribed to Shan-tao describes man's plight in terms of a traveller pursued by wild beasts and highwaymen, running desperately until he comes to a great river. On the one side of the river great flames are roaring, on the other side mighty waves are raging. Before him there is only a narrow, white road between the flames and the waves. Halting irresolutely he hears the voice of Sakyamuni Buddha encouraging him: 'Go' and the voice of Amita Buddha from beyond the river crying: 'Come! I will

1. *The White Lotus Ode*, tr. Karl Ludwig Reichelt, *Truth and Tradition in Chinese Buddhism*, 1934 ed., p. 127.
2. C. H. Hamilton, *Buddhism: A Religion of Infinite Compassion*, New York, 1952, p. 125.
3. *Shinshu Seiten*, p. 248.

protect thee.' With new faith in his heart, he presses forward.

Pure Land Buddhism means, then, faith in Amita's saving vow, a faith which is of such consequence that in this tradition Sakyamuni Buddha, the founder, may seem to take second place to Amita Buddha. At the same time it is frequently observed that

> To trust in Amita but means
> To trust in all Buddhas.[1]

The accent on faith becomes, if anything, even more pronounced with the further development of Pure Land teaching and practice in medieval Japan. Following the scholarly reformer, Honen, with his 'only repeat the name of Amita with all your heart' there is the devoted Shinran, founder of the popular Shin sect, the Martin Luther of the new movement, who, leaving the cloister and taking to himself a wife, announced a Way which a farmer may follow as well as any monk. Everything in this Way depends, not on man's achievements, but upon Amita's gift of faith, a gift which is freely made –

> Walking or standing, sitting or resting, I mind little of time or space, be it defiled or not. What there is is that single adamantine faith, that consciousness of His Grace, that gratefulness that I feel towards the Master of the Way.[2]

At the end of a long life Shinran writes to some of the country people who have walked many miles to visit him in his retirement at Kyoto that he is convinced that the Jodoshinshu teaching which he has done so much to establish is 'the utmost end of Mahayana Buddhism'.[3] Others may

1. *The Shinshu Seiten*, p. 208. cf. p. 86, 'To meditate on the light of the Buddha of eternal life is to "see all the Buddhas".'
2. Kosho Yamamoto, *The Private Letters of Shinran Shonin*, Tokyo, 1936, pp. 31, 32.
3. ibid., p. 6.

very well say the same, though perhaps with different meaning, as they observe the distance between this Buddhist 'religion of grace' and the Theravada teaching which offers no 'other help' except the Buddha's example and teaching, names no Amita and knows no Pure Land. The diversity of belief and practice is indeed so great, not only between Theravada and Mahayana traditions, but within the Mahayana tradition itself, that again the question is raised of the significance of such umbrella terms as Mahayana or Buddhism. Can they be said to refer to anything which may be described as a total context of life and thought? Is there really such a thing as a fundamentally Buddhist outlook shared by members of all the different Buddhist sects or schools? How far can a man go and remain a Buddhist?

Interwoven with such questions, there are questions regarding the Pure Land religion in particular. What is the significance of the comparison which is drawn when, together with certain forms of Christian and Hindu faith, Pure Land faith and practice is named a religion of grace? Does such a religion of grace really belong to Buddhism? Is it a description which might be anticipated when it is observed that even in the Theravada tradition the Bodhisattva conception is not entirely absent though overshadowed by a conception of Buddha as the Sage? Or should we look behind or beneath the doctrinal terms and conceptions to the underlying religious experience? Can we discern in all the major traditions two types of religious experience, one associated with an optimistic view of human nature, its conditions and capacities, and the other taking a more pessimistic and desperate view, emphasizing human need as the heavens are scanned for signs of a rescuing saviour? On this latter view it might perhaps be concluded that this second kind of experience will push its way through, so to speak, and demand expression wherever man walks the earth in whatever religious tradition he may be nurtured so

THE STUDY OF RELIGIONS

that doctrine becomes shaped accordingly, even when the context of the particular faith, viewed as a whole, might seem unfriendly as in the case of a Buddhism which begins with such a strong emphasis on self-help.

Discussion of these and kindred issues returns us to the question raised earlier in these pages as to whether Buddhism can indeed be considered as a whole or as a total context of life and thought gathered round some one central affirmation. One of the new facts of our day is a Buddhist oecumenical movement comparable with the Christian oecumenical movement and one of the leaders of this movement, Dr Malalasekera, states roundly that it is wide of the truth to conceive the two great schools, Theravada and Mahayana, as 'two hostile camps'. On the contrary, members of both traditions from many lands have found that they can 'meet in complete harmony in spite of the difference in their views'.[1]

What then inspires this harmony? Some may point to certain fundamental and distinctive doctrines, such as the doctrine of Dependent Origination and the *an-atta* doctrine, however variously they may be interpreted. Others may refer to the analysis of the human condition affirmed in the Four Noble Truths and the consequent emphasis of the one Path leading to the one goal, nirvana.

The answer suggested by our discussion of Theravada Buddhism was that the central reference is the Buddha himself. In the beginning Buddha: his story, his life, his teaching, exhibiting a certain character with its twin virtues of wisdom and compassion which all his followers seek to emulate. It is clearly more difficult to maintain this thesis when we come to the Mahayana tradition. The difficulty here is not so much that the Buddha is 'glorified' as the fact that he is manifold. New names appear until finally there is

1. G. P. Malalasekera and K. N. Jayatilleke, *Buddhism and the Race Question*, UNESCO, 1958, p. 10.

a name Amita who to all intents and purposes seems to take the place of the historic Buddha of the Sakyan clan. There may still be a Buddha story, but it is a different story along with different scriptures. Yet, when all is told and all allowances made for this rich diversity, the kind of character which a Buddhist tries to realize, whether he thinks of it in terms of his own potential Buddha-nature or in terms of the example of Gotama, remains the same. There may be perhaps, in the Mahayana tradition a greater emphasis on the virtue of compassion but this same compassion is again and again said to mean the exercise of skilful and appropriate means which depend on a Buddha wisdom. Whether the accent be on faith or on one's own resolution or on both, the character to be realized remains the same and to realize this character is to attain nirvana. To know one Buddha, it is repeatedly said, is to know all. To know one or to know all, it might be added, is to seek to have the mind of the Buddha. It is this central purpose and reference which holds the Buddhist world together.

The Tradition of Islam

WHEN it comes to the youngest of the world's great religions, the religion of Islam established by the Prophet Muhammad in the Arabian desert in the seventh century A.D. which today numbers over 450 million adherents, the need for western reappraisal arises from the fact of proximity rather than distance. Islam has been a near and alarming neighbour. Hence western misunderstanding may be attributed to prejudice as well as to ignorance.

The new understanding which has come with the disappearance of much of this prejudice has meant, among other things, a better appreciation of the name Islam. If it is disparaging to name this religion the sect of the Saracens or the religion of the Turks, it is just as objectionable from the orthodox Muslim standpoint to use the name Mohammedanism, for Muhammad cannot be regarded as the founder of the Muslim faith in the same sense as Christ is regarded as the founder of the Christian faith. The appropriate name, it is held, is Islam, a name which signifies submission to the will of God. To suggest otherwise is to obscure the reference to divine revelation which dominates the Muslim outlook.

Nevertheless, from the historian's standpoint, Islam begins with Muhammad and the first step taken in western reappraisal has been to give Muhammad his due. Earlier western caricatures which portrayed him as a religious lunatic, or an arch heretic or, at best, a reformer who began well and became a scheming politician and a debauched sensualist, have been succeeded by tributes to Muhammad's remarkable leadership, genius, and character. Christian writers among others today refer to Muhammad's single-minded devotion, nobility, stature, and uniqueness,[1] the 'sincerity of his piety'[2] and his humanity.[3]

While such statements are partly due to new freedom from prejudice, however, they are also partly due, as in the case of other traditions, to new knowledge. There is new knowledge, for example, of Muhammad's Arabia. The Mecca of the seventh century where Muhammad was born and where he taught is seen today as no mean city. It was a thriving commercial town at the juncture of caravan routes crossing the Arabian desert.

It was also a religious centre renowned throughout Arabia. The Ka'bah sanctuary in the heart of the city attracted many pilgrims. It reflected the complex pattern of Arabian paganism, a paganism best described as a nature worship verging on polytheism, a worship which included the veneration of sacred stones, natural phenomena, and particular places associated with divine powers or agencies. The pilgrims who came to the Ka'bah from all parts of tribal Arabia might have special regard for the famous Black Stone set in one of the walls of the central building. This was an object of immense veneration. But there were many other sacred stones in the Ka'bah as also the shrines of the three goddesses of Mecca, Al-Izzat, the goddess of power, Manat, the goddess of fate, and Allat, the goddess of fertility. There was also some recognition of a supreme Being named Allah, the creator of heaven and earth. It was this naming of Allah which gave Muhammad his starting point –

If thou ask them who hath created the Heaven and the Earth ... they will certainly say, 'Allah'. ... If thou ask them who

1. Kenneth Cragg, *The Call of the Minaret*, pp. 94, 101.
2. Tor Andrae, *Muhammad, the Man and His Faith*, tr. p. 185.
3. H. A. R. Gibb, *Mohammedanism*, 2nd ed., p. 33.

THE STUDY OF RELIGIONS

sendeth rain from Heaven and by it quickeneth the earth ...
they will certainly answer 'Allah'. (XXIX, 61, 63)[1]

Muhammad therefore had no need to argue for the
existence of Allah and he did not do so. What he emphasized
was the reverence due to Allah. The worship of Allah, he
argued, should be the only worship. All other worship was
idolatrous.

Nor was he the first to maintain this view. Besides men-
tioning Jews and Christians, 'the people of the Book', the
Qur'an refers to an obscure, pre-Islamic tradition of monotheism represented by the so-called Hanifs, who believed
that Allah was the only God and apparently shared Muhammad's conviction that Allah and none else was the Lord of
the Ka'bah, the 'Lord of this house' (CVI).

Neither the name Allah, then, nor the belief in one
supreme deity, was entirely new to Arabia. Nevertheless,
the Hanifs seemed to be comparatively few and far between,
the Jews and Christians were aliens, and the great majority
of Muhammad's fellow countrymen in Mecca and beyond
Mecca were pagans in practice and belief. The Ka'bah in
Muhammad's day was the citadel of a confused idolatry.
While, therefore, Muhammad could appeal to a vague
belief in one supreme God named Allah, he was something
more than a reformer. He was not merely calling upon men
to be logical and put into practice what they already
believed. To all intents and purposes, the faith he preached
meant a parting of the ways. It challenged the whole
complex of pagan belief wedded to tribal custom which
found expression in the Ka'bah rituals as well as the
privileges and profits of the Meccan guardians of the
shrine. The measure of the man, therefore, must be
taken in the light of the measure of the force of this challenge, the resistance it was bound to arouse, and Muham-

1. Sura XXIX, Qur'an. References to the Qur'an in pages following are indicated similarly.

mad's achievement despite this resistance. He found an Arabia which merely looked over its shoulder at Allah and left an Arabia for whom Allah was all in all, the First and the Last.

Some two hundred miles to the north of Mecca there was Yathrib, a small desert oasis later to be known as Al-Medina, 'the city'. In the year A.D. 622 Muhammad, accompanied by his stalwart companion, Abu Bekr, fled secretly from a Mecca which had turned against him and crossed the desert to Medina. With this event, afterwards known as the migration, the Hijra, Islamic history began. In the ten pregnant years which followed there were to be skirmishes in the desert between the men of Mecca and the men of Medina which later generations of devout Muslims would regard as the first engagements in Islam's holy war – a war which was to bring Muslim armies as far west as the straits of Gibraltar in less than a century and establish a dominion in the name of God reaching far beyond Arabia.

No religious history has been more dramatic nor more improbable at the outset. By observers at the time these skirmishes in the desert might well have been dismissed as of no particular consequence. They followed a familiar pattern. Caravans were intercepted and plundered, tribesmen were slain or captured, together with their womenfolk and children, and the booty taken back to Medina. Observers, however, might have viewed things differently if they had listened to Muhammad after one of these raids –

O true believers – it was not you who slew those who were slain at Bedr. It was God who slew them. . . . O prophet, stir up the faithful to war: if twenty of you persevere with constancy, they shall overcome two hundred, and if there be [only] one hundred of you, they shall overcome a thousand of those who believe not; because they are a people who do not understand.[1]

1. Sura VIII, believed to have been dictated by Muhammad at Medina after the battle of Bedr.

'O prophet, stir up the faithful.' It was the presence of the Prophet which made this little war between Mecca and Medina different from other wars in the desert – Muhammad's presence, his personality and his deep and strong conviction that all that was now happening was by divine decree. It was this same conviction passed on to his devoted followers which was to mean in the years to come an Islam spread across the map of the world like a huge splash of ink with its centre in Mecca, splashed westward through Egypt and North Africa as far as Spain, northwestward to the Balkans, northeastward to Persia, India, China, and splashed southward through Malaya to Indonesia. Much of this territory was to constitute Muslim empire with its several kingdoms ruled by princes who shared the belief of the Prophet that all was by divine decree, the decree of Allah, the one, the only God, the Lord of men, the King of men.

At the time of these early skirmishes in the desert, however, any prospect of Mecca ever becoming the centre of such a Muslim world might have seemed very dim indeed. Except for a few faithful followers mainly drawn from the poor and menial, the men of Mecca had rejected him. From their own standpoint, they had done so with good reason. Muhammad had not only denounced the profitable idolatry which attracted pilgrims to the Ka'bah shrine. He had announced principles which implied, as will be seen, drastic social and political changes threatening the vested interests of the Meccan oligarchy.

Muhammad was born in Mecca and he grew up there, taking part as a young man in its caravan trade. It was not until he was well in middle life, however, that he claimed to be the Prophet of Allah, sent to warn men of divine judgement.

According to tradition he was an orphan from boyhood, brought up by a kindly uncle, a member of a comparatively poor but respected Meccan family. A verse in the Qur'an recalls this situation –

Did He [God] not find thee an orphan and give thee a home?
And find thee erring and guide thee? (XCIII, 6)

Is it going too far to read between the lines of this verse and see a boy who, like other boys in similar circumstances, was more introspective and thoughtful than most, the boy who was to become the Muhammad who took to wandering the hillsides outside Mecca, making his way to the cave on Mount Hirah where he would sit for long hours, strangely disturbed, strangely expectant? One night, in this same mountain cave he had the dramatic experience which changed the whole course of his life. It is told that while he slept the angel Gabriel came to him bidding him: 'Recite, thou, in the name of the Lord who created man from clots of blood.' It is also told that when he awakened from his sleep and came out of the cave – 'and it was if they had written a message on my heart' – he saw the angel 'at the far horizon of heaven' and he heard a voice saying: 'O, Muhammad, thou art Allah's apostle and I am Gabriel.'

He was now a married man, having married the wealthy widow Khadijah, fifteen years his senior, when he was twenty-five; and none stood by him more loyally than Khadijah in the days which followed. He had the more need of this support because at first he was agitated by many doubts. What had really happened? These voices he had heard and continued to hear, were they the voices of evil spirits bemusing him? Was he out of his mind, as some of those around him were quick to suggest?

The angel spoke to him again:

I swear by the morning brightness
By the night when it grows dark
Thy Lord has not forsaken thee. (XCIII)

And again:

> O Prophet
> Proclaim that which thou hast been commanded.

What Muhammad thus felt himself commanded to proclaim was, he insisted, no new doctrine. It was in fact
essentially the same message of divine judgement as that
which had been proclaimed by the prophets of Israel and
Muhammad himself conceived it to be a message as old as
the human race. He referred to a great succession of prophets sent by God to proclaim this same message, naming
Moses, Jonah, John the Baptist, and Jesus among them,
giving his own version of stories told in the Bible. Did he
derive this knowledge mainly from Jewish sources, as was
formerly supposed, or mainly from Christian Syriac sources
as is now concluded? However this question may be
answered, it is evident from the Qur'an that Muhammad
himself claimed direct inspiration. The fact that he did so
in answer to the charges of forgery brought against him
indicates the opposition he encountered. It began with ridi-
cule, but it soon became more serious. While Muhammad
himself was protected by his Hashimite kinsmen, some of
his poorer followers, including slaves, were beaten and
tortured. Seventy of them fled to Abyssinia.

He had other followers, however, besides menials and
slaves. There was, for example, Umar, the future Caliph. It
was Umar who was Muhammad's companion on his flight
to Medina and it was Umar, a man renowned for his up-
right character and spartan simplicity who, after Muhammad's death, succeeded the first Caliph, Abu Bekr, and,
himself unspoilt by success and uncorrupted by power,
directed the advancing power of Islam as the Muslim army
marched from victory to victory. If any famous ruler in
history deserves to be called 'great', observes the Danish
scholar, Tor Andrae, it is Umar.

Can the same be said of Muhammad himself? The very fact that Muhammad could attract to his cause such forceful characters as Umar and Abu Bekr is surely testimony to Muhammad's own force of character. But it has often been alleged by Muhammad's critics that whatever nobility of character he achieved in Mecca, he lost when he went to Medina. The passage to Medina, it is said, meant a deterioration of his character and a change in his purpose ... At Mecca, Muhammad was the Prophet. At Medina, he became the scheming politician, primarily concerned with defending and establishing the new Muslim community which he founded there. It is with particular reference to this criticism that the first step in our modern western reappraisal of Islam has been taken.

As to any change in Muhammad's purpose, it will presently be noted that the very substance of his message implied community. It was implicit from the first in all that he taught about the divine sovereignty and human responsibility. New study of the Qur'an has made this plain as also new study of the significance of the whole development of Muslim law. But we are also pointed to the same conclusion by noting some of the steps Muhammad took before he went to Medina. It was not just a question of seeking asylum. He went there by invitation and he was preceded by some seventy of his Meccan followers. He also went there on his own terms and he delayed his departure until these terms were accepted. The inhabitants of Medina included two rival Arab tribes and a Jewish colony. There had been prolonged and bitter feuds between the two Arab tribes. Men from Medina who had visited Mecca and heard Muhammad preach had been impressed by his character and personality. They urged him to come to Medina and restore peace and order. Muhammad welcomed the invitation as one that would give him opportunity to do at Medina what he had thus failed to accomplish in Mecca.

But he did not accept the invitation until he was assured, not only that his rule would be respected, but that there was prospect of the kind of community he had in mind. He obtained from the men of Medina pledges to abandon idolatry, theft, adultery, fornication and infanticide. 'Nor', they promised, 'will we disobey the Prophet in anything that is right.'

Arab community was tribal and one of the first steps taken by Muhammad after his arrival in Medina was to establish a new community cemented together by the bond of a common faith in place of the old tribal bonds. He arranged that each one of his followers brought from Mecca should enter into a personal, fraternal bond with a tribesman from Medina. 'Only the faithful are brethren.' (XLIX, 10.) A mosque was built and it was later decreed that the faithful, when they prayed, should turn their faces towards Mecca, Mecca with its famous Ka'bah sanctuary now given to idolatry but meant to be, as Muhammad saw it, the house of Allah.

Such regulation is significant. It indicates both the early development of the new community, the congregation (*umma*) of Islam set alongside the tribes and the Jewish congregation of Medina. It is regulation which goes beyond anything attempted at Mecca. But it also suggests previous planning. There is a possible argument here against the view that Muhammad's new legislation was merely dictated by immediate necessity. There was certainly necessity enough, for the situation at Medina was precarious. It was only a small oasis town and there was urgent need to provide food for his followers and the growing population. Hence the raids in the desert and the plunder of caravans bound for Mecca.

None of his contemporaries would have condemned Muhammad for such raids. They would have done the same in similar circumstances. But when one of these raids occurred during the month which was observed by Arabs as a time of truce, there was an immediate outcry, and here, it has been charged, Muhammad was open to criticism on more than one account. Besides the charge that he failed to observe the truce, it is charged that he dissimulated and attempted to put the blame on a subordinate when the raid aroused an outcry among the Arabs in Medina. Later critics have charged him with inventing alleged divine revelation to suit his convenience when he announced that Allah had revealed to him that while it might be reprehensible to fight in the month of truce it was even more reprehensible to cease to strive in the way of God. (II, 214)

Similar criticism of Muhammad's alleged invention of new revelations when it suited him has been made with regard to his private conduct. His devoted wife, Khadijah, died before he left Mecca and at Medina he took unto himself not one wife but several, until there were twelve women in his harem. One of these, Ayesha, is said to have taunted him when he resorted to dubious stratagems to introduce a new lady to his harem and claimed that Allah had revealed his approval. 'Truly', said Ayesha, 'the Lord makes haste to do thy pleasure.'

Muhammad's harem has been one of the things which has most prejudiced western opinion against him. It is taken by Muhammad's critics as sufficient proof in itself that his character deteriorated. The Prophet of Mecca urging men to follow in the straight path, it is said, became a self-indulgent sensualist. Most western writers today, however, brush the criticism aside with some impatience. Muhammad must be seen, they say, in the light of his own accepted norms of conduct, and it is not surprising that he accepted the polygamy of his clime and day. What is rather cause for comment is the fact that in the regulation of his new community he sought to improve the position of women, as is evident from the many references to the subject in the Qur'an.

Much the same attitude is taken in regard to Muhammad's public conduct. Granted that he was putting into practice in Medina what he had preached at Mecca, then allowance, it is urged, must be made for the difficulty of attempting such practice. It was no simple task to form his Arab tribesmen into a new community which had also to be defended against attack from Mecca and sabotage from within Medina itself. Criticism of Muhammad's shifts and wiles is qualified therefore by tribute to the qualities of leadership which he demonstrated, the resolution which he manifested, the remarkable defence which he contrived when Medina was besieged and the way in which he marshalled the forces which were to bring him back to Mecca in final triumph before his death. Tribute is also paid to his statesmanlike magnanimity towards his opponents in his hour of victory.

There is the greater need to recall this magnanimity when Muhammad's harsh treatment of the Jews at Medina is remembered. Here perhaps we have the most serious indictment of all. Despite the Prophet's efforts to win them to his side, the Jewish colonists in Medina remained aloof. After the siege of Medina, Muhammad not only resented their hostility; he was apprehensive; he was afraid that they might turn against him and become an enemy within the gates. But he had to proceed with caution. These Jews had formerly been allied with one of the Arab tribes. Muhammad therefore arranged that a member of this tribe should decide their fate. He knew very well, however, what the decision would be, for the particular tribesman delegated for the duty was one of his most fanatical followers. The harsh verdict was only what was expected; the merciless execution of all the men in the colony and the slavery of their women and children. Such cruelty and trickery is scarcely met by the plea of political or military expediency. It is more convincing to claim, as might indeed be claimed, that his conduct on this occasion was out of keeping with the humanity and magnanimity Muhammad showed at other times.

It is still more convincing to say, as Muhammad himself might have said, that, after all he was human – a very great human maybe, this astonishing leader of men, who, after eight strenuous years returned to Mecca in pilgrimage and victory, captain of an army of ten thousand men, yet still the Prophet – a very great human, but no more than human. And here we touch on a point which is important for our understanding, not only of Muhammad himself but for the faith which he proclaimed, the faith which is Islam. If the first step taken in the western appraisal of Islam has been to give the Prophet his due, the second step taken has meant that the Prophet is given *no more than his due* or the due which he himself would have claimed.

What has been called the creed of Islam consists of two main articles:

> There is no God but Allah.
> Muhammad is His Apostle.

'His apostle' – but no more. Thus from the Muslim standpoint, if Muhammad is named the Christ of Islam as some western writers have suggested, his status is exaggerated and violence is done to the first article of their creed. There are indeed some Muslim statements which might be quoted in support of such a comparison, for there is more diversity in Islam than is often supposed and in course of time a Logos doctrine meant a conception of Muhammad comparable with the Christian conception of Christ. But the great majority of Muslims would repudiate any such view:

The Prophet Muhammad was but a man, of a purely human

THE STUDY OE RELIGIONS

nature. He was neither a great God, nor a small God, nor a sub-God, nor even an auxiliary of God. . . . The Prophet led us into the light of truth . . . but however great our respect for him may be . . . he is not raised above the level of man . . . he was God's Apostle and servant.[1]

If there is any Christ in Islam, it is not Muhammad but the Qur'an. The message comes first, Muhammad second. In other words, Truth, God's Truth, is prior to prophecy – the heavenly Truth attesting divine sovereignty and judgement, then a 'sending down' of this Truth in divine mercy and compassion.

To the non-Muslim 'the original Qur'an' is the book written in Arabic consisting of over a hundred chapters or suras (of very unequal length) giving the substance of what Muhammad taught in Mecca and Medina as recalled by his followers just after his death. But to pious Muslims 'the original Qur'an' is a 'heavenly book'. It is the transcendent pattern of Truth, God's Truth, communicated to Muhammad by the angel Gabriel. Muslims have debated whether this heavenly Qur'an is eternal as God is eternal, but none have questioned the belief that the teaching contained in the book (*kitab*) originated, not in Mecca, nor in Medina, but in Heaven. It is this teaching to which we must now turn, and to do so should mean a better understanding of why, from the Muslim standpoint, Muhammad must be given his due as *the* Prophet, yet not more than his due.

The main theme of the Qur'an is divine revelation. No religion takes this theme more seriously than the religion of Islam. It is expressed in three cardinal doctrines. There is first the doctrine concerning the source of revelation, the doctrine of God; secondly, the doctrine concerning the agents of revelation, the messengers of God, angelic

1. Mohammed Abd Allah, 'Draz, The Origin of Islam' in *Islam – The Straight Path: Islam Interpreted by Muslims*, ed. Kenneth W. Morgan, New York, 1958, p. 40.

and human; and thirdly, doctrine concerning the recipients of revelation, man who will be held responsible for his conduct at the day of judgement.

The doctrine of God begins with the affirmation of divine unity. The very name Allah emphasizes this unity. It is the shortened form of *Al-ilāh*; *the* God –

> God
> there is no god but He, the
> Living, the Everlasting
>
> . . . .
>
> His Throne comprises the heavens and earth
> He is the All-high, the All-glorious (II, 256)

It is a unity which must never be denied or obscured by any statement or action which might seem to attribute 'partners' to God. To do so is a 'monstrous sin' (IV, 51). Western writers, however, have sometimes presented this statement of divine unity in a way which disregards the fact that there is equal emphasis on divine *action*. For Muslims, Allah is emphatically 'the living God' who is both utterly transcendent, beyond all human conceptions, yet, at the same time manifestly concerned with human history. He is 'the First and the Last, the Manifest and the Hidden' (LVII, 3). He exists from all eternity and all depends on Him. 'All things perish, except His Face' (XXVIII, 88). The creator of the heavens and the world, His will is sovereign. All is by divine decree. 'God leads astray whomsoever He will, and He guides whomsoever He will' (LXXIV, 34). Terrible in His power, His majesty, and His judgement, He is yet provident and bountiful, the compassionate and the merciful. The Qur'an insists again and again that the divine providence and bounty should be plain to all if they would only look around them and observe the wonder of nature –

> It is He who stretched out the earth
> And set therein

Firm mountains and rivers,
And of every fruit He placed there two kinds,
Covering the day with the night.
Surely in that are signs for the people who reflect. (XIII, 3)

While there is a main emphasis on the divine transcendence
there are also verses which suggest divine immanence and
a mystical indwelling of God, including the verse, frequently quoted, that God is 'closer to man than his own
neck vein' (L, 15).

Important as it is, however, for Muslims to acknowledge
that there is only one God, the omnipotent creator who
determines all things according to His will, it is equally
important for them that His will has been made known.
Nothing said therefore about the manifestation of God in
Nature is considered to obviate the need for the special
divine communication which is emphasized in the second
major doctrine, the doctrine which has to do with the
messengers of God, angelic and human. It is this doctrine
in particular which illuminates Muhammad's status.

First there are the angels. There is frequent reference in
the Qur'an to the great company of angelic beings, 'the
honoured servants of God' (XXI, 26), who support the
throne of God, record the deeds of men, receive the souls
of the dying, guard the gates of hell and witness for or
against men at the last judgement. As 'the protecting
friends of man' in this present life and in the world to come,
the angels also come to man as God's appointed messengers (XXXV, 1). They support the believer in the straight
path. And he has indeed need of this support, for besides
the angels he is surrounded by other invisible beings, the
jinn, some of whom are evil, intent on seducing men (VI,
129). There is also the satanic tempter named Iblis, a fallen
angel.

But man is doubly warned against such evil. Besides the
angels, God has chosen messengers from among mankind

itself. The Qur'an names a great succession of human prophets. The message they have brought is fundamentally the same:

Say (O Muslims): We believe in Allah and that which is revealed unto us and that which was revealed unto Abraham, and Ishmael, and Isaac, and Jacob, and the tribes, and that which Moses and Jesus received ... We make no division between any of them. (II, 130 ff.)

The reference to the Old Testament patriarchs and to Moses and Jesus reflects the Muslim view that Jews and Christians are in a special category. Like the Muslims, they are 'people of the Book'. But another verse implies an even wider announcement: 'there is not a nation but a warner has passed among them' (XXXV, 24).

Muhammad comes within this same prophetic succession. He is indeed the last of the succession, the very seal of the prophets, 'completing God's favour' (V, 5). But in himself he is no different from other human messengers of God. He is no Christ. He is 'only a mortal' like his hearers (XVIII, 111) –

Say: 'Glory be to my Lord! Am I aught but a mortal, a messenger?' (XVII, 95).

This last statement comes at the end of verses which emphasize the marvel of the Qur'an. Muhammad's hearers want proof of his authority. They ask for a miracle. He replies that the message he has brought is proof in itself. The message, the Qur'an, is miracle enough. 'If men and jinn banded together to produce the like of this Qur'an, they would never produce its like' (XVII, 90; X, 38). All the emphasis is on the fact that such a message has been given and secondly that it has been given through Muhammad: 'God has sent forth a mortal as Messenger' (XVII, 95). Such is Muhammad's status and it is status enough; the status of a prophet; the status of the prophet, bringing a final warning and bringing it to the men of Arabia specifically.

Hence these same men of Arabia, these hearers in Mecca, can be held accountable for what they do in response to this message. Doubly warned by angelic and human messengers and now finally by Muhammad, they must stand doubly at the service of God (as the pilgrim to Mecca reminds himself to this day). This is the third main doctrine announced in the Qur'an, a doctrine gathered around the recurring symbol of the last judgement. The day will surely come, the Day of Doom (LXX, 25), the day when 'the earth shall be changed to other than the earth' (XIV, 45), the day when the trumpet will sound and the dead will be raised and all men will return to God (XXIII, 100 ff.), the day when men will keep tryst with God from whom there can be no escape (XVIII, 55 ff.). No excuses will avail on that day when man is 'told his former deeds' (LXXV, 10). The true believers will be separated from the unbelievers who will enter the gates of hell while the believers enter paradise, the garden of eternity (XVI, 30; XXV, 15).

Death, then, means for the Muslim a homecoming to God the creator who has given man certain opportunities and capacities and will judge him accordingly. Man *is* accountable to God. That is the very nerve of Islamic faith and practice. It means that in the final analysis man is regarded as a free and responsible moral agent. There are indeed passages in the Qur'an which are hard to reconcile with this emphasis on human freedom and responsibility. What for instance are we to make of the statement which insists that God leads astray whomsoever he will and guides whomsoever he will (LXXIV, 30) or what, again, of the statement that God lays veils upon the hearts of men lest they understand his message (XVII, 45; XVIII, 55)?

There is certainly a problem here for the theologian, a

problem which attends all doctrines of divine predestination, whether Muslim or Christian, or, for that matter,
all religious statements which emphasize divine sovereignty
on the one hand and human freedom on the other. It was
a problem which was to vex the minds of Muslim theologians in the years to come. But Muhammad was a prophet, not a theologian. His message, with its recurring
symbol of the Last Assize, was intended to leave his hearers
in no possible doubt that they were called upon to prepare
themselves for judgement to come. Whatever limits might
be set to human freedom by divine decree, they had freedom enough within these limits to decide their own fate.

Far from being a fatalistic religion as is sometimes supposed, Islam has thus been a religion marked by a strong
sense of human responsibility for human conduct. It is an
individual responsibility. 'God charges no soul save to its
capacity. Standing to its account is what each soul (itself)
has earned' (II, 285). 'No soul (so) laden bears the load of
another' (XVII, 15; LIII, 39). Muhammad never offered
to shoulder this load. He was not a saviour. His task was
to call man to observe the 'straight path'. But he did come
with guidance in regard to this straight path and for this
praise belongs to God. To God! Not to Muhammad. For
it is the fact that this guidance is God's guidance, now
specially communicated, that is all important. God is the
shattering reality with which men must come to terms.
That is the resounding theme of the whole Qur'an and
Muhammad's status, function, authority and significance
all derive from the fact that he is the spokesman of this
God. In the final analysis all that has been done is God's
doing and the conclusion is reached that in response to
this doing, in submission, there must be man's doing. Such
is the sequence. First God, then the Messenger, then the
insistence on human response.

While the responsibility is individual it is a responsibility for social duty. The message was spoken to Arab tribesmen who lived in tribal society, each tribe with its own traditional 'custom' (*sunna*) regulating the conduct of the tribe, providing them with guidance. To have taken such tribesmen out of society, leaving each to go his own individual way, would not have been something for which to praise God. Muhammad's message therefore meant new regulation, new guidance, new *sunna*. Thus Muslim religion from the beginning has been regulated religion, with order seen as Heaven's first law. And this regulation has spelt community, as the Qur'an makes very plain. Believers are to 'help one another to piety and God fearing' (V, 1). They are to do righteous deeds

> and counsel each other unto the truth
> and counsel each other to be steadfast. (CIII)

Sinners in hell are portrayed as deserving their fate because they 'were not of those who prayed and (they) fed not the needy' (LXXIV, 45). True believers, on the other hand, while 'performing the prayer' are 'to pay the alms' (LXXIII, 15 ff.). As they 'continue at their prayers' they are also mindful of the rights of the beggar and the outcast (LXX, 25). Most of these verses, it may be noted, are quoted from chapters which are generally considered to record the teachings given in Mecca. They anticipate the fuller and more precise regulation contained in the later, Medina statements which contain prescriptions and prohibitions covering a wide range of subjects from food and drink, marriage and divorce, to the bequest of property, usury, and behaviour in war; prohibitions having to do with what may break community and prescriptions having to do with what may maintain it. Thus religious observance throughout the Qur'an is linked with social duty.

Among these regulations are four in particular which hold believers to the straight path, mindful of the divine will. They have been called the pillars of faith. First it is enjoined that there must be daily prayer, secondly, alms giving, thirdly, fasting, especially during the month of Ramadan, and fourthly, pilgrimage. These might be named the four religious duties except that in Islam no hard and fast line is drawn between religious and social duty. Variously worded, there is the constant insistence –

O believers, be you securers of justice, witnesses for God. . . .
. . . .
Be equitable. . . .
And fear God; surely God is aware of the things you do. (V, 10).

To read the Qur'an, then, is not only to see Muhammad as the agent of divine revelation. It is also to conclude that what is thus revealed, and hence regarded as sent down from heaven, is a pattern of human conduct, individual and social, which means new community in accordance with the divine will. As Allah was named the Lord, the king of men (CXIV), so it might be concluded that Islam was intended to mean God's kingdom on earth. And this intention is plain from the first Meccan messages. Thus from the Qur'an we have answer to the charge that Muhammad departed from his vocation as prophet when he departed for Medina. On the contrary, it might be held that all that he did in Medina in founding a new community he did in fulfilment of this vocation. There was no inconsistency.

Muhammad, it has been claimed, was a very practical prophet, and Islam has been a very practical religion. Jesus (wrote the distinguished Muslim jurist, Syed Amir Ali) was put to death before his work was finished. Had he lived longer he would have placed his teachings on a more systematic basis. It was therefore left to the prophet Muhammad to do what Jesus was unable to accomplish. 'The glory of

Islam consists in having embodied the beautiful sentiments of Jesus into definite laws.'[1]

But even Muhammad, it might be observed, did not live long enough to provide all the legislation which was required. After the prophet's death, questions began to arise which could not be answered by reference to the Qur'an alone. To meet this need, the Qur'anic rulings were supplemented by reference to traditional Arab practice (*sunna*). As further questions arose there was reference to rulings and traditions handed down from first-generation Muslims with particular regard to guidance given by the Prophet himself as recalled by his companions. It was felt that these constituted a clarification of what was implicit in the Qur'an. The collection of traditions referring back to the Prophet himself (*hadith*) was the first step taken towards the great corpus of Law (*shari'a*) which is one of the most distinctive features of Islam.

As time passed, however, and extended dominion called for extended law, it became evident that recourse to precedent or tradition was not enough. There was no avoiding the exercise of rational judgement although Muslim scholars were very cautious about any such exercise. Here we have an early instance of that tension between reverence for divine revelation and respect for human reason which has been characteristic of Islam throughout its history. Valuing above all else the divine guidance which came to them with divine revelation, Muslim scholars looked now for some similar guidance in their development of their great system of law. They were dubious about any recourse to what might be regarded as purely human judgement. The majority of them found this guidance by reference to the 'consensus of the community' (*ijma*). The Prophet, it was believed, had foretold that his community 'would never agree in error'. Agreement therefore signified truth.

1. Syed Amir Ali, *The Spirit of Islam*, London, 1935, pp. 170–3.

But it might also be held to signify continued divine guidance through the community which owed its very existence to such guidance. In point of fact, the consensus sought was generally the consensus of scholars versed in the Law, who could be regarded as speaking for the community. And among Shi'a Muslims especially there was a respect for private judgement which qualified appeal to consensus. As already observed, Muslims have their differences and these have existed from the beginning and to a greater extent than is often realized. Early disputes regarding the leadership of the community led to a main sectarian division between Sunni Muslims, who compose the majority, and Shi'a Muslims who, generally speaking, have claimed greater liberty of opinion. Nevertheless, one of the most remarkable things about the Muslim world has been its solidarity, and the great system of Muslim law has certainly contributed to this solidarity. The pride of Islam, the system of Law, has also been very much the strength of Islam.

To bring others within the pale of this same beneficent Law might seem a pious Muslim charity and an argument along these lines has sometimes been advanced in defence of the practice of holy war (*jihad*). Against the objection that Islam's wide dominion was only achieved at the point of a sword, it has been replied that the conquered had good reason to welcome this dominion. 'We like your rule and justice', the people of a Syrian town are reported to have told their Muslim conquerors.[1] But whatever might be said for and against such an argument it has not, in point of fact, been Islam's main ground for engaging in holy war. Here again we are taken to what is fundamental to Muslim thought and practice: the reference to divine sovereignty. The Qur'an enjoins holy war, and by some Muslims it has been regarded as a fifth 'pillar of faith'. It may at least be

1. Philip K. Hitti, *History of the Arabs*, New York, 1937, p. 153.

THE STUDY OF RELIGIONS

seen as an expression of faith: the faith that Allah's rule must be proclaimed and extended. According to this reading, holy war is never, in intention, war for the sake of aggression. The Qur'an expressly forbids aggression. 'God loves not the aggressors' (II, 186). But the Qur'an in this very same passage expressly exhorts believers to fight 'till there is no persecution and the religion is God's'. In another passage the question is put: 'Will you not fight people ... who purpose to expel the Messenger?' (IX, 10–14). Islam's first battles, then, may be seen as battles to overcome the opposition to the Prophet's witness and the subsequent wars as wars undertaken to maintain and extend this witness. Whatever benefits to mankind may have resulted from the extension of Muslim dominion, the main consideration and dynamic motive has been the conviction that God's rule must be proclaimed, His sovereignty respected, His will obeyed. Hence there must be liberty of prophesying, without let or hindrance, and if the only means to overcome let or hindrance is the sword, then the sword must be taken. Such is the argument.

Thus the Islamic community appears on the pages of history as a community inspired by a body of very clear-cut convictions expressed in a body of clear-cut law. As such it is certainly a tradition of special interest to the student concerned with the function of religion in society. It calls a sharp halt to any attempt to reduce religion to something other than religion or explain religious ideas as no more than the reflection or product of social conditions and patterns. While due allowance may be made for political and social factors in the shaping of Islamic society, the starting point and the continuing dynamic is religious conviction. The shaping of society in line with such conviction follows. That is the sequence. If there had been no Muhammad deeply persuaded of a divine mandate to fashion human society in accordance with revealed norms, a Muhammad able to convince his followers that this was indeed the case, the whole pattern of Muslim community would have been different.

For the historian, Islam is no less interesting and for similar reasons. The story of Islam through the ages brings into further relief the force and effect of religious convictions definitely affirmed and strongly held. If Islam has taken divine revelation seriously, it has also taken its own history very seriously and for fairly obvious reasons. No one can fail to be impressed (and, least of all, Muslims themselves) by the spectacular achievements of the first classical period of their history, the period of Arab expansion symbolized by the building of the new city of Baghdad on the Tigris in 762 A.D. The Mongol invasions meant a change in Arab fortunes and a period of crisis symbolized by the fall of Baghdad in 1258. But as the new conquerors embraced the faith of the conquered and Ottoman sultans succeeded Arab caliphs, there began a second great period of Muslim achievement and expansion scarcely less remarkable than the first, with Islam taking new forms in Persia and Turkey. Thus Islamic community has been as Professor Cantwell Smith puts it, 'community in motion'.[1] For close upon a thousand years Muslims exercised a very large say in the shaping of world history. The fact that today, while still pursuing their missionary advance in Africa, they no longer have such a decisive influence poses a problem. From the Muslim standpoint 'something has gone wrong with Islamic history.'[2]

Something has gone wrong with history because history, as Muslims conceive it, is threaded by divine purpose and Muslims have manifestly been the agents of this purpose. God has been on their side. But in modern times an

1. Wilfred Cantwell Smith, *Islam in Modern History*, Princeton, 1957, p. 18.
2. ibid., p. 41.

invasive Islam has itself been entered by an invasive western world. Under the changed political conditions of today some Muslims may very well ask whether God is any longer on their side and some, perhaps, whether Muslims are any longer on the side of God.

When it comes to the philosophy of religion, the grounds for interest in Islamic faith are perhaps not so apparent. Western philosophers have not shown anything like the same interest in Islamic thought as they have shown in Hindu thought. Their interest in Islam has been largely confined to the role played by Muslim thinkers such as Averroes in reviving the western study of a forgotten Aristotle. The very fact that Muslim statements are so clear-cut may repel interest in Islamic thought itself. 'It makes me shiver!' exclaimed an American scholar after listening to an exposition of Islam by a Muslim visitor who was nothing if not definite and forthright. Rightly or wrongly, she attributed his clarity to superficiality. She missed the hesitation which she associated with philosophic wonder and inquiry.

It is here, perhaps, that there is still need for fuller understanding on the part of non-Muslims. Mistaken conclusions can very easily be drawn from the sharply edged patterns of Muslim belief and practice. The constant naming of God and the frequent reference to the divine will may produce the impression that not only Muslim life, but God Himself is reduced to pattern and fully presented in a few concise dogmas. But such a notion is, in fact, entirely foreign to the pious Muslim. His very respect for divine revelation is joined with the thought that only so can God be known. In His ultimate majesty God transcends human thought, and what He has made known is not His own secret being but His will for mankind. Muslim teaching concerning the divine being is therefore qualified by a reverent agnosticism which, strange as it may seem, invites comparison with Buddhist agnosticism. When it comes to some ultimate questions there is the same silence, the same concentration on knowledge pertaining to the Path or the Way man must follow. There is also special regard, as in the case of Theravada Buddhism, for the teacher who brings knowledge of the Path. In this respect at least, Gotama the Enlightened One and Muhammad the appointed Messenger fulfil the same function and the result in each case is fidelity to an authoritative scripture which prescribes a way of life while it still leaves man wondering.

Of wonder, whether it be named philosophic or poetic, there is certainly full measure in the Qur'an –

In the Name of God, the Merciful, the Compassionate
By heaven and the night-star!
And what shall teach thee what is the night-star?
The piercing star!

(LXXXVI)

By the white forenoon
and the brooding night!
Thy Lord has neither forsaken thee nor hates thee (XCIII).

As to inquiry, philosophical or theological, here again there is need for western review. It will mean taking greater account than is often the case of the full range of Islamic expansion, eastward as well as westward, and the significance of such developments as Sufi mysticism, poetry and speculation.

It will also mean observing that while fidelity to divine revelation imposes restraints, the content of revelation as recorded in the Qur'an poses questions which could scarcely fail to flex the minds of intelligent believers. A good many of these questions are familiar enough to the West, for Islam, not without reason, has been described by some as Christian heresy and by others as Calvinism overheated. It may seem therefore that Islam offers no new prospects and this presumption may discourage interest.

Nevertheless, the theologians of Baghdad lived in a different world from the theologians of Geneva and western wits may be stimulated by discovering what Muslim thinkers made of such a subject as divine over-ruling and human freedom. If all is by divine decree in what sense can man be held responsible for his own fate?

This was one of the issues which agitated the minds of the first Muslim scholastics, the Mu'tazilites. Repudiating the extreme position of those who maintained rigid doctrines of predestination, the Mu'tazilites proclaimed themselves 'the supporters of Divine Unity and Divine Justice'. And the support they proposed was quite definitely the support of reason. Their familiarity with Greek, Jewish, Christian and Zoroastrian thought stimulated them to examine the why and wherefore of divine justice. Allah must be *just*, as he was also compassionate. It was in accordance with this justice and compassion that he sent down the truth contained in the Qur'an in response to human need. Hence the Mu'tazilites rejected the view that the Qur'an was eternal, existing before such need. They added, moreover, that such a view set the Qur'an itself over against God. It was incompatible with the conception of the divine unity.

Like all other Muslims, the Mu'tazilites acknowledged the primacy of the Qur'an. They could scarcely have remained within the Muslim fold if they had not done so. But respect for the Qur'an, they believed, was not only compatible with human reason; it called for the exercise of human reason. Nothing which was contrary to reason could be regarded as true. Therefore the Qur'an could not be held to affirm anything contrary to reason, and appeal to reason could not be construed as infidelity to the Qur'an.

The Mu'tazilites also came to believe that the depth of truth contained in the Qur'an could only be realized if some of its statements were not taken literally. Allah, infinite and eternal, did not actually sit upon a throne supported by angels, nor could believers be said to *see* God when they attained paradise. Such language, if taken literally, implied a divine being bounded by time and space. The promised vision of God should rather be construed as a vision of the *bounty* of God. The language was figurative.

Mu'tazilite speculation, however, aroused the increasing alarm of other Muslims. Simple believers felt that their heaven was being taken away from them if they could not expect to see God when they reached paradise. Conservative scholars objected that the omnipotent God who plainly commanded obedience was being replaced by philosophical constructions. Rejection of Mu'tazilite conclusions, however, did not mean rejection of the Mu'tazilite appeal to reason. Al-Ashar and other theologians employed rational demonstration to confute the Mu'tazilites' views in defence of what was generally regarded as orthodox opinion. There was lively debate. Indeed, far from there being no theology in Islam there was theology enough to cause public demonstrations and riots in Baghdad.

The Asharite theologians had popular opinion behind them. God was inscrutable and if it was difficult to reconcile predestination with human freedom that was only due to the limitation of human wit. God had made His will plain enough and man had accepted that will, entering into covenant with God when the children of Adam, as stated in the Qur'an, testified: 'Yes, God was indeed their Lord and they would be accountable on the Day of Resurrection' (VII, 171). Reason might be employed in the defence of the faith but the limits of this employment were set by divine revelation.

There were others, however, besides the Mu'tazilites who seemed disposed, according to more conservative Muslims, to go beyond these limits. While the Asharite system became the recognized theology of most of the Sunni Muslims, the various Shi'ah sects held to esoteric doctrines reflecting neo-Platonic and Asiatic thought.

There were also the Sufis. If a more favourable presentation of the Prophet has been one of the features of the western reappraisal of Islam, much the same might be said in regard to the Sufis. The tendency in the past has been to regard the Sufis as very much on the fringe of Islam. They have been narrowly identified with a mysticism which seemed foreign to the true genius of Islam or with the kind of extravagance exhibited by fanatical dervishes. Today, however, they are more generally seen, with their emphasis on religious experience, as constituting the very nerve of religious life in Islam.

The Sufis probably began as small groups of humble, devout believers concerned to maintain the earlier Islamic piety against the temptations of new wealth and power which came with the establishment of Muslim empire. Wearing simple garments of white wool (*suf*) – hence the name Sufi – they may have been influenced by the asceticism which they observed in the Christian monastic orders. As the centuries passed they founded similar orders themselves, each with its own religious leader, and they established monasteries or convents, although for the most part they were not celibates. Dispersed throughout Islam, the Sufi movement took different forms as it enlisted Muslims of different sects, and some of the Sufis were just as essentially orthodox, if not more orthodox, than other Muslims. From the start, however, there was a tendency towards mystical speculation. The Sufi mystics could claim that there was no need to go beyond the Qur'an itself to justify this tendency. Together with the divine transcendence, the Qur'an affirms divine immanence, proclaiming the God who is 'near to answer the call of the caller when he calls' (II, 182), the God who is 'closer to man than his own neck

vein' (L, 15). There were versions of Sufi mysticism which
approached sheer pantheism. Zeal for union with God led
the martyr, Mansur al-Hallaj, crucified for alleged blas-
phemy, to exclaim

Betwixt me and thee there lingers an 'it is I' that torments me.
Ah, of thy grace, take this 'I' from between us.

The great Sufi poet Jalal al-Din Rumi, 'intoxicated with
Love's cup', professed

I have put duality away, I have seen that the two worlds are one
One I seek, One I know, . . . One I see, One I call.

Besides the Shi'ah and the Sufi speculations there were
the great rationalistic systems constructed by a succession
of the Aristotelian philosophers including al-Farabi,
Avicenna and Averroes.

It is generally held that al-Ghazali won the day for
orthodoxy in the eleventh century and that thereafter there
was no more intellectual ferment in Islam. But al-Ghazali,
writes a Muslim scholar of the present day, 'is a most
difficult author, if not an outright impossible one, to understand in any coherent manner . . . he began to write esoteric
treatises in which he admits philosophical doctrines which
he rejects in works meant for the public.'[1] Al-Ghazali was
certainly scathing in his criticism of 'the incoherence of the
philosophers' but he was also more than indulgent of the
Sufis. In fact he himself became a wandering Sufi. He spent
eleven years in retirement, engaged in meditation and he
died in a Sufi convent. Al-Ghazali was certainly no cold
intellectual. Writing on the love of God, he rebuked those
who 'deny the possibility of . . . any intimacy with God, or
passionate longing for Him.' If his writings in general
buttressed orthodox opinion, they also encouraged more
tolerant attitudes towards Sufi piety. It is doubtful if he
would have viewed with any favour the stereotyped

1. F. Rahman, *Prophecy in Islam*, London, 1958, p. 94.

scholasticism which came to prevail in the Sunni colleges established in city after city before the end of the fourteenth century.

It is the same tepid scholasticism which western writers have had in view when they have concluded that Islam's intellectual vitality reached its terminal point in this period. But the Sunni colleges were mainly in the West and Islam had travelled eastward as well as westward. If account is taken of the tradition of the illuminationists which developed in Persia and beyond, it might be held that the advent of al-Ghazali did not mean an end to philosophy in Islam but rather an end to a particular kind of philosophy. The spell of Aristotelian rationalism was broken. But it was followed, at least in Persia, by a new philosophical movement which may be broadly described as neo-Platonic. The founder of this school, the Persian sage al-Suhrawardi, a Muslim thinker virtually unknown in the West until recent times, is quoted by Seyyed Hossein Nasr as testifying

Our sayings have not come by means of rational demonstration but by inner vision and contemplation ... Whoever is traveller on the road to Truth is my companion ... The procedure of the master of philosophy and imam of wisdom, the Divine Plato, followed the same path.[1]

The works of this 'companion of all travellers on the road to Truth' had a profound influence on the thought of Shi'a Muslims, especially in Persia. Translated into Sanskrit and Hebrew they also influenced Hindu and Hebrew thought.

Professor Nasr observes that at the same time that Aristotelianism was becoming known in the West through the works of such Muslim scholars as Avicenna and Averroes, 'it was being rejected as a completely rationalistic system in the Islamic world'. He makes the interesting suggestion that

1. Seyyed Hossein Nasr, *Three Muslim Sages*, Cambridge, Mass., 1964, p. 63.

the parting of the ways between the two sister civilizations of Christianity and Islam after the seventh to fourteenth century can be explained in the role that this rationalistic philosophy was to have in the two civilizations.[1]

Some may think that Professor Nasr exaggerates the influence of eastern Muslim thought. But when it comes to what may be contributed to the philosophy of religion such an issue is immaterial. What is more to the point is the vitality of the thought expressed, however wide or narrow the range of its influence. As it may be concluded that there is more diversity of thought and practice in Islam than is sometimes recognized, so also it may be concluded that there is more intellectual vitality in this tradition than has sometimes been realized.

When it comes to the philosophy of religion, however, it is not just a question of noting how much or how little of philosophy there is in this or that particular tradition. Even if it could be shown that there has been no 'intellectual fervent' in Islam itself, which is certainly not the case, Islam might still be presented as intellectually exciting. It is exciting, for example, in its attitude to evil. The whole conception and practice of holy warfare implies a sensitivity to evil as something which is more than any absence of good, something which has to be resisted and overcome in a resolute 'striving' against all that is not holy. Far from being a submissive fatalism, the faith of Islam which has shaped human history appears as a faith which posits resistance to a Satan as well as obedience to a resolute God. At the same time it is a faith which has nurtured mystics who profess that 'the secret of all created things ... is clear, and thou dost not see in this world or the next aught beside God.'[2]

1. ibid., p. 54.
2. Ibnu al-Arabi quoted by Sidney Spencer, *Mysticism in World Religions*, London, 1963, p. 311.

PART TWO

Philosophy in the Meeting of East and West

I

PHILOSOPHY has played a very important part in the development of the great religions over a long period. It will be evident to anyone who knows anything about Christianity how much this religion has owed, for example, to Greek philosophy. Nor can any informed person doubt the place of philosophy in Indian religions. Hinduism and Buddhism had extensive philosophical elements within them almost from their earliest known history, and there has rarely been a time when the philosophical element has not been prominent in those religions. Much that is maintained about God in Islam and the Islamic conception of revelation has depended much on the work of philosophers who also incidentally had a great deal to do with the course of thought and culture in Christendom. Chinese religions, in spite of their dominant concern with practice, have had as their background distinctly philosophical notions, like those involved in the concept of Tao, which have had a formative influence on the ways of life they commend. In a developing culture, and in our present state of sophistication, philosophical thinking about religion becomes more than ever an integral part of the true life of religion and a condition of its effective renewal and perpetuation in a form we can wholeheartedly acknowledge and find adequate to the needs of our times at all levels.

This is not however a view which will find very general endorsement today. It will be firmly rejected in more than one quarter. Theologians will be conscious of the harm done to the cause of true religion by the rash confidence of liberal thinkers in the nineteenth century and early in this one when they sought to give an exhaustive account of distinctively religious notions in terms of the exceedingly rationalist form of Hegelianism which prevailed then. This set up a vigorous reaction which not only recalled religious thinkers to the need to make very full acknowledgement of the transcendence of God but also induced them to interpret this notion, or its implications, in the form of an extremely irrationalist and deliberately paradoxical theology which paid little heed to the standards of consistency which philosophers normally consider it their business to safeguard. 'What has Athens to do with Jerusalem?' it was asked of old, and the sentiment has been passionately reaffirmed in our time. We shall return to it later.

It is not however solely from without the domain of philosophy itself that resentment of its intrusion upon the sphere of religion and theology has been voiced. Many philosophers have expressed similar views. This has been for various reasons. Prominent among them is the general supposition that philosophy in fact never affects in any important way the matter with which it deals. It is a secondary activity valuable entirely on its own account. It makes no difference of note to anything outside itself.

This view has been very widely held of late, and I must now hasten to add that I consider it to be as mistaken as any view can be. The sphere in which it seems most plausible to say that philosophy makes little difference to the subject it studies is that of our knowledge of the external world. We may agree, let us suppose, with Berkeley in holding that material things only exist in being perceived. But this makes no difference at all to the way we treat material objects or live in the world around us. To hold a view like that of Berkeley is not to suppose that the objects around us are unreal or illusory in a sense which means that we need take no account of them. Berkeley was himself the first to correct such an impression and to insist that his theory accorded closely with common sense. We start in philosophy from what we find our normal experience to be like, and if any view requires us to disregard our normal perceptual experience that makes the theory profoundly suspect at once. There have indeed been views which hold that material realities, indeed all individual and historical existence, are altogether unreal. But these seem to me among the most implausible of all philosophical speculations.

At the same time philosophical notions can make some difference even to our attitude to physical objects in the world around us. To revert to our former example, namely Berkeley's view of the external world, it is hard to see how anyone could hold that view with real understanding without being properly impressed at the remarkable dovetailing of our perceptual experiences, within the experience of one individual and in the relations of that to the experiences of others, into one another within the corpus of our perceptual awareness. There is thus induced a sense of wonder and respect which may well affect in subtle ways even our most mundane treatment of material objects. Some similar result might follow if we came to the conclusion that mind and matter were coterminous in the universe or if we held, as again in the case of Berkeley, that material objects depended on the mind of God or in some other way but thinly veiled the reality of God as the sustainer and author of all things. We might in these ways acquire what is sometimes described as 'a sacramental' view of matter and this would make some difference to the way we treat material objects.

At the other extreme we might have a view, like that of Plato, in which material realities are trivial and unimportant and the sensuous satisfactions they bring not worth much attention or integral at all to the fulfilment of ourselves in other ways. The philosophical views of Plato have had much to do with the subsequent cultivation of ascetic attitudes and the renunciation of the world, especially in respect of material goods and satisfactions. A good deal besides theories of perception is involved here, but they play their part; and the most that I want to do here is to give some indication of the way a philosophical view may help to determine the attitude we adopt even towards material things.

I find it harder to determine whether the philosophical investigation of the nature and method of other intellectual disciplines can affect the course which those disciplines take. Does the philosophy of science influence the way science is studied? Some philosophers would certainly say 'No', and this reply would be echoed by many scientists. They do not, they would say, need the philosopher to teach them their job, the philosopher has his legitimate curiosity and is helped and encouraged to satisfy it, but his conclusions have nothing to do with evidence, or the marshalling of evidence on which the particular findings of science depend. This might however be too simplified a view, and it would be a little odd at least if the philosophy of science were, as most would admit it to be, an important branch of philosophy today and have effect in no way at all on the way scientists go about their work. We might say the same about history. No historian needs the philosopher at his elbow all the time, and many would be much hindered if they had had to be thinking of some kind of philosophical mentor or critic looking over their shoulders. Some very outstanding historians have been very inept or mediocre philosophers. In some cases the concern with a philosophical theory has been a snare and a hindrance to gifted historians, and in the light of that one might well be tempted to say that the best thing for the historian is to get on with his own job and let the philosopher mind his – even in the philosophy of history. On the other hand, it is in fact unlikely that philosophical views about history, as these come to be widely held, have no general effect on the attitudes of historians to their work. There are after all considerable diversities of opinion among historians themselves as to the way their subject should be studied, and it is not difficult to detect some incipient philosophical notions about history and about the world in general implicit in much of these differences. A determinist could come to the study of history in a very different way from someone who believes that human beings can in some very absolute way shape some features of their own destinies. Much of the history written in the nineteenth century, some of it written by authors who were themselves eminent philosophers, as in the case of T. H. Green, was extensively affected by Hegelian idealism. Then there are the crucial questions of relativism and bias in history. It seems certain to me that the attitude adopted in these respects by the practising historian can have much influence on his work. If he inclines to a relativist view, and even more if he holds that view strongly he might well not take all the pains he should to ascertain the truth and limit the influence of such bias as is inevitable. The views held about religious truth could also have much influence on the way a historian examines certain sacred texts and the conclusions he advances. This subject is a vast one in itself, and here I only touch the fringes of it; and I can therefore only give it as my own opinion here that the philosophical investigation of the nature of history and its methods can have importance, not only for the general significance we ascribe to history, but also for the day-to-day work of practising historians.

I am certain that moral philosophy can make a difference to our ethical attitudes. Those who resent this suggestion assume that it authorizes the philosopher to determine directly for us our way of life or to prescribe our ethical standards and evaluations for us. That is certainly not the work of the philosopher as such. A philosopher may not always be the best person to consult about some practical problem. But however firmly we maintain this, there seems to be no doubt that the clarification of ethical notions by the philosopher can have a far-reaching influence on our practical attitudes and decisions. Take the simple distinction between the actual results of an action and what the agent himself intends. An action may have untoward unforeseen consequences, but in enlightened cultures we would not take the agent himself to task for this. We would judge him on the basis of his intention. What happens beyond that, provided he has done his best, is not in his control. But this has not always been understood and there have from time to time been savage judgements against an unfortunate person for consequences of his action which he could not have anticipated. Primitive morality tends to look in this way mainly at the outward deed, and in times of confusion civilized people tend to lapse into the same barbarous attitude. A further distinction which has been sharpened and made prominent in philosophical thought about ethics is that between the act which is really right, what the situation truly requires, and whatever a person at the time takes to be his duty. The more we bear this distinction in mind the more we shall cultivate a wise tolerance in dealing with people who act on convictions sharply opposed to our own. We realize that though we may sometimes feel impelled to oppose or hinder such people, sometimes by harsh measures, we must not think ill of them as moral agents since they are doing the only thing they can properly do in the circumstances, namely abide by the light they have. In a similar way we are brought to appreciate the fallibility of our own judgements and thus to take greater pains to try to make our opinions on moral matters as sound as they can be. Closely related to this is the insistence on individual rather than collective responsibility. Here again our enlightened attitudes may be confused through the persistence within them, or the resurgence in times of disturbance and upheaval, of primitive attitudes. There have in this way also been savage persecutions of innocents, as in the treatment of the Jews under the Nazis. Primitive peoples think mostly in terms of the tribe or the family and there are certain ways in which the thought of later times has been prone to various confusions which encourage the same procedure. A sound ethical analysis can help us to think clearly on such questions and thereby extensively affect the way we behave towards one another. Reflection on the content of our duties and the way we establish this, normally and in cases of perplexity, can also have a marked effect on what we do in various situations. Our attitude to capital punishment for example could be extensively affected by whether or not we believe in retributive punishment; and the question of keeping a certain kind of promise (such as the promise given without witness to a dying man) could depend a great deal on whether we consider a promise to have at least some binding force in itself, or can be thought to depend entirely on the good consequences of keeping promises and the undermining of confidence, and kindred ill-effects, due to breaking a promise.

There are also philosophical systems in which ethics, far from having any autonomy of its own, is thought to be derived from some more basic principles governing the world as a whole. The ethics of Spinoza is bound up closely in this way with his metaphysics. This does not seem to me to be warranted, but even so one has to recognize here again a case where the advice we would give or accept on some question of practice could be substantially affected by the philosophical ideas we adopt.

It will also be evident that we cannot disentangle certain aesthetic attitudes and procedures in artistic or literary criticisms from ideas which appear in the first instance in the context of philosophical thought about art. Tolstoi was fortunate in that his ideas about art did not much hinder his work as a creative writer, but in other cases, notably in some of the work of Wordsworth, the literary activity has been seriously marred through the ill-effects of faulty general notions about art.

Philosophy, then, can make a considerable difference in some ways to the activities or other subject matter which the philosopher investigates, and I believe that sound philosophical thinking can not only prevent us from falling into misleading errors or provide us with illuminating distinctions, but in other ways extend our sensitivity and deepen our experience in such matters as aesthetics, ethics, or the pursuit of science. The notion that philosophy influences nothing beyond itself is the product of a very negative and narrowly formal conception of the task of philosophy current today but little in accord with the main ways the subject has generally been studied or the more impressive achievements of those who have pursued it.

This is particularly true of religion. Mention has already been made of the prominent part played by philosophy in the life of the great religions. I do not think it as significantly absent from other religions as many suppose, and this is a subject that cries out for closer investigation today. If the philosophical views involved are mistaken, then there will be something radically wrong at the very core of the religions themselves. It seems thus particularly hard to divorce philosophy from the study of religions, and I think many who set themselves to that task, have been seriously hindered in their work by failure to have sufficiently subtle grasp of the philosophical issues in the material they study.

This brings me to a matter of considerable current importance. There have recently been marked advances in the study of oriental languages and a new mastery of the techniques they require. With this has gone much refinement of oriental scholarship in general. This makes the expert in those fields very jealous of the high standard of scholarship which his subject may boast. He is apt to resent the intrusion of other scholars into a field where they do not have the competence of the linguistic expert. This is very understandable. But it has also considerable danger, namely that of the technical expert establishing for himself a monopoly of the study of many-sided cultures which require much for their understanding besides specialized linguistic knowledge. This is an area of study where the close co-operation of many scholars seems to be pre-eminently required. Even when we seem to be dealing with severely factual issues or with scientific questions our understanding of how certain practices appeared, in respect of their ultimate meaning and significance, to those who observed them can be of the utmost importance; and that is an area where the philosopher has much to contribute. If the linguistic expert complains that the philosopher intrudes upon a domain where he is lacking the necessary tools, the philosopher can make the corresponding claim about the technical expert. In any case, no one can have the same expert mastery in all important fields of linguistic study. One expert must learn from another and rely on the most authoritative opinion available in fields where human frailty and limitations of time preclude his being an expert himself. Judicious cooperation seems to be the appropriate policy, and in some respects the insights of the philosopher appear to be the essential pre-requisites for the soundest understanding of features of various cultures and religions of the world.

This is exceptionally true at the present time. For not only have there been many advances in the scholarly study of religions, and exciting new findings, but also considerable sharpening of insight in the philosophical understanding of religion. This has far-reaching importance for Christian theology and the commendation of Christian faith today. Much in traditional Christian theology is very difficult to accept in the light of modern scholarship and the more sophisticated culture which is inevitable for us now. Some of the basic affirmations of the faith sound strange in modern ears. This has led some thinkers to jettison, not merely incidental features of Christianity which can plausibly be thought to be solely due to the thought forms of the first century and earlier Hebrew times, but also essential doctrines, as they still seem to many, about the work of Christ as redeemer and, as a historical figure, a reconciler of the world with God. Others resist all change and stand firmly by dogmatic doctrinal affirmations or some kind of Biblical fundamentalism. It seems to me, however, that we should take neither of these alternatives and that if we consider the essentials of the Christian faith afresh in the light of understanding of religion available to us now we can see more clearly than ever how firmly established they are and how strikingly significant they become in the situations in which we find ourselves today. I shall touch on this theme again, but as I have been much concerned with it in other books, I shall devote the greater part of this essay to showing how much our understanding of other world religions is enhanced when we approach them with the refinement of our understanding of religion attained in recent years. This will give us a point where philosophy has a great deal to do with the meeting of East and West in the world of today generally, and it is with that in mind that we can now work our way deeper into our subject.

II

There can be little doubt in the mind of any thinking person today about the permanent importance of understanding between East and West, and between the inheritors of different cultures in various parts of the world. At the social and political level this is peculiarly obvious and is being forced upon us in the exigencies of events which are rapidly developing and becoming fraught with grim possibilities which are filling our minds with uneasy forebodings of disaster. We are not directly concerned with these social issues in this essay, and it is for the statesman, not the philosopher, to discover the practical measures and institutions by which the sources of power and communication available to us now may be made the means of closer cooperation and friendliness throughout the world. But it is also evident that political understanding is not to be achieved and made permanent without understanding also at the cultural level, where the habits of mind and dominating interests of peoples are formed. We have heard much of late about social engineering, and contemporary thinkers in the West have perhaps been a little too impetuous in adopting these quasi-mechanical concepts of social existence. This may well prove one of the points where a due infusion of the calmer wisdom of the East may enable the West to view its new conceptions in their proper perspective. It is in any case evident that there is a very important cultural side to the social questions which bewilder us today; and, in addition, new advances in scholarship and new insights have made it plainer than ever how valuable in itself, as an enrichment of experience, is a fair appreciation of one another's cultures.

It is here that recent philosophy has, in my opinion, a very distinctive contribution to make, but it is not altogether along the lines laid down by those who shared the same ideals in the last century.

As is well known, the treasures of eastern philosophy were not made readily available to the West until translations of notable texts began to be made by Anquetil-

Duperron and later by others in the nineteenth century. Occasional and sporadic exchanges there had been, and in many subtle ways the philosophies of the East and the West have affected one another to a greater extent than used to be thought. But it was not until the last century that eastern philosophy came to be extensively and fairly reliably known in the West; and this was the period also when western philosophy made its greatest impact in India and other eastern countries, where western philosophy became an important item in the curricula of new and expanding universities.

It was not surprising that this should lead to high-minded attempts to discover the factors common to the philosophies of the East and West, and, on the basis of these, to lay claim to an impressive underlying identity. This procedure had much to encourage it at the time – the optimism of the nineteenth century, for example, and the belief in progress, together with the spread of a liberal and tolerant attitude of mind. But what seems to have prompted it most of all was the dominant position of idealism as a philosophy. Idealism, in this context, means the view that reality is one whole or system of such a nature that the inevitability of its being what it is presents itself as a rational necessity – in other words, everything is bound to happen as it does because of its place in a system which is rationally self-explanatory. For our limited minds the explanation might not always be forthcoming, but we could always see the principle of it and know that there is nothing which will not eventually admit of a complete, rational explanation. For anyone able to view the system as a whole there would remain no element of mystery nor any feature of existence which we had just to accept or take for granted. The text for this was the dictum of Hegel: 'The Real is the Rational and the Rational is the Real.'

It is not easy for us today to appreciate the confidence

with which this view was held as recently as the first half of the present century. We have lived through a period of profound disillusionment and have had to reckon with irrational factors in our experience well calculated to depress any confidence we have about the prospect of providing a thoroughly rational explanation of all things. We have perhaps swung to the other extreme and now underestimate the place of reason in life. But that, for the moment, is another story. What we need to remember now is that, in the latter decades of the nineteenth century, philosophers generally had an unbounded confidence in idealism in the sense indicated and they assumed that this would remain the prevailing philosophical view for all time. All that was left for the future was to refine the formulations of idealism and apply them more effectively to particular problems.

This confidence in reason and the belief that the universe is one whole or system found a ready response among leading eastern philosophers. This was due in part to the western training which many of them had received and their proneness to read their own classical texts, the Vedanta for example, through the spectacles of western idealism. But the initiate will also readily appreciate that there really are important points of affinity between the monism of the Vedanta and idealism, and that many forms of Hinduism could fairly easily blend with the idealist tradition. The notion, present in much western idealism, that all things, as we encounter them, are unreal, or illusory, being only real in their place in the one Absolute Whole, has a great deal in common with the belief in the illusory or unreal nature of our present existence as it appears in more than one eastern religion. Nor is the affinity confined to general principles. For there is a great deal in Hindu and Buddhist philosophy that has its origin in preoccupation with subtle difficulties about our knowledge of the external world such as western philosophers study as the subject called 'perception'. Students of perception in western countries are far from appreciating properly what extremely suggestive work, some of it of a closely technical character, has been done, in remote times and in quite recent studies, by eastern thinkers.

The gentle accommodating habit of mind on the part of eastern and western philosophers has, however, suffered many rude shocks of late. For one thing, the erstwhile confident system-building idealist philosophy has fallen upon evil days. It has been very largely abandoned in Europe and America. This is due partly to penetrating criticisms of the main principles of idealist philosophy, but in many cases idealism is left high and dry, in favour of various forms of empiricism, without careful, much less sympathetic, scrutiny of its claims. I think this extremely unfortunate, not because I favour an idealist philosophy myself, but because I believe we have much to learn from it which is most sadly neglected today. That is, however, too long a story to tell now. But the fact is that, in English-speaking countries, all forms of metaphysics and system-building have been extensively discarded as wholly unprofitable enterprises, and have been superseded by the so-called philosophies of positivism and linguistic analysis; while, in other places in the West, the movement known as existentialism seems to hold the field.

Among the pioneers of the philosophy of analysis were G. E. Moore, Bertrand Russell, and Ludwig Wittgenstein. Of these it is Moore who made the most direct attack upon idealism, but it is probably Wittgenstein who has had the most considerable influence in setting the prevailing philosophical fashion.

The substance of this so-called revolution in philosophy was this. It was argued (or assumed) in the first place that nothing can be true or even meaningful unless it can be understood in terms of experience, the latter being thought of exclusively in terms of sense experience or emotional states. This in itself is not very new. It was the position of Protagoras, for instance, among the Greeks, and was subjected to searching examination and criticism by Plato. In modern philosophy it had its supreme exponent in David Hume. Hume seems to be the patron saint of most western philosophers today, and according to the out-and-out empiricism he advocates there can be no true or even meaningful assertions about the soul as an abiding entity, about objective moral standards or about God and immortality. Beliefs about these sorts of things have to be jettisoned as containing nothing but 'sophistry and illusion'.

A story about an influential Oxford professor brings out well the shift of interest and attitude in philosophy in the early part of this century. The professor was asked by a distinguished Indian visitor: 'And what do they think about immortality in Oxford these days?' – and he gave the abrupt reply: 'We haven't heard of it for the last twenty years.'

Along with an uncompromising acceptance of out-and-out Humeian empiricism and its inevitable scepticism there appeared a new technique designed to dispose of ideas like the soul or God and immortality. This technique was known as linguistic analysis, and it took the form (at first at least) of ascribing the apparent meaningfulness of statements about, let us say, the soul, to linguistic confusion. The statement 'the soul is immortal' sounds a possible one because it has a normal grammatical form and thus gives us the delusion of speaking meaningfully. But in fact it is in the same class as the statement 'gravity runs faster than virtue', which is of course just nonsense. Metaphysics thus came to be regarded as nonsense by which people allowed themselves to be deluded.

Into the close and ingenious ways in which these procedures came to be commended, and into the finer and more cautious developments of this kind of philosophy, I cannot enter now. But it is evident that it accords ill with attempts to bring all the varied facts of experience and facets of culture under some one comprehensive scheme or principle in which differences of outlook ultimately disappeared or ceased to give trouble. Students of religion, directly or indirectly influenced by the prevailing philosophical fashion, have been increasingly inclined to confine themselves as closely as possible to reporting alleged facts without attempting to press beyond them to some underlying unity. We are to be told how people bury their dead at different periods and places, how they build temples, what form their ritual takes and so forth; but what this carried with it further in the way of belief or inner experience is thought to be too treacherous a ground to venture upon.

This change of attitude has certainly some important merits. It has brought us down to earth from some rather vague flights of undisciplined metaphysical fancy, and it has brought much common sense to our studies. We are no longer so prone to overlook disconcerting differences in people's intellectual attitudes and cultures, or to treat opposing convictions and practices as of little account by comparison with some alleged underlying unity. We are more cautious and not so ready to allow high-minded enthusiasm to obscure awkward facts and genuine differences; and in this we have no doubt learnt much from the unhappy course of recent world events which have shown us that distressing and stubborn differences are not to be wished away or resolved by dwelling piously on the glories of an imminent millennium.

A most effective illustration of this change was the inaugural lecture delivered by Professor Zaehner on his appointment to the Spalding Chair of Eastern Religions and Ethics at Oxford. Succeeding Radhakrishnan, who has brought his wealth of learning and profound insight to the task of interpreting the East and the West to one another, Professor Zaehner sounded a much more cautious note in warning us not to set aside too lightly the undoubted differences of belief and practice which appear in the religions of the world. He declared:

Thus to maintain that all religions are paths leading to the same goal, as is so frequently done today, is to maintain something that is not true.

Not only on the dogmatic, but on the mystical plane, too, there is no agreement.

It is then only too true that the basic principles of Eastern and Western, which in practice means Indian and Semitic, thought are, I will not say irreconcilably opposed; they are simply not starting from the same premises. The only common ground is that the function of religion is to provide release; there is no agreement at all as to what it is that man must be released from. The great religions are talking at cross purposes.

It is therefore foolish to discuss either Hinduism or Buddhism in Christian terms; and it is at least as foolish to try to bring the New Testament into harmony with the Vedanta. They do not deal with the same subject matter. Even Indian theism is not comparable to Christianity in a way that, for example, Zoroastrianism and Islam are; nor are the various avatars of Vishnu really comparable to the Christian doctrine of the Incarnation.[1]

It is possible, however, to be unduly cautious and down to earth, as we shall see. Some western philosophers, in a healthy reaction against the excessive and occasionally facile optimism of their idealist predecessors, seem to have swung to an even more vicious extreme by repudiating all forms of speculation altogether. The time now seems to be ripe for putting the lessons learnt from the philosophy of analysis, and its often disconcerting techniques, to a new purpose in the form of a constructive philosophy which shall essay afresh the task of seeing how things look as a whole

1. *Foolishness to the Greeks*, O.U.P., 1953.

or unity – the traditional task of philosophy. Increasingly philosophers are coming round to this view and wondering what the future has in store for us now that we turn again to metaphysical problems fresh from our bath of linguistic analysis and common-sense philosophy.

It is here at this vital growing point of contemporary western philosophy, that the impact of eastern thought, both ancient and modern, can be peculiarly fruitful, much more so, I am sure, than western philosophers generally realize.

This is partly because these twin theses of sceptical positivism and constructive metaphysics appear to have been much more subtly intertwined in eastern thought than has been the case in the West, where rival philosophies alternated and opposed one another more sharply. But this in itself is closely bound up with certain insights into ultimate problems which have a peculiar relevance to the present state of western philosophy.

III

This shows itself most clearly in regard to the way we should think about God. For one of the most important results of the so-called challenge of recent empiricism has been that philosophers and others have been compelled to consider again how they must think and talk about God. Many have contended, for example, that the idea of God is essentially absurd. They do not mean merely that the evidence against there being a God is overwhelming, as one might deny that there is a man in the moon or that Napoleon won the battle of Waterloo. They mean that to think of God is to try to conjure up an impossible idea like that of a square circle. For some this is just a consequence of a strict empiricism. They take it for granted that nothing can be meaningful if it is impossible to reduce it to empiricist terms, that is to what we experience through our senses. But others take the attack further than this. They claim that, over and above the requirements of an empiricist outlook, there are further radical difficulties in the idea of a divine being.

These appear especially when we think of God as an absolute or necessary being. It does not seem possible for instance to qualify an absolute being, we appear to limit Him if we do so; but if we do not qualify a being in some way it seems hard to identify Him or regard Him as any kind of reality. It is likewise difficult to see how anything can exist by necessity. We find necessity in proportions like those of mathematics or logic. But we know that things exist by finding that in fact they do, not by seeing that they are bound, being the sort of things they are, to exist. They could just as well not exist, and if we refer to their antecedents, as in some way requiring that they should be, we have to admit that particular causal relations are again what we find to be the case and that it is not unthinkable that the causal relations of things should be other than they are. If, moreover, we try to establish the existence of God from any consideration of what we find the world around us and our own experience to be like, we seem to be left with an entity which is less than God, if God is thought to be an absolute or necessary being. To reason from any particular features of experience to some reality that would account for them is to posit a qualified reality, some entity with the particular characteristics that would account for these distinctive facts; we establish, not an ultimate unconditioned being but one term in a system of relations, one entity among others.

Variations on the theme of these difficulties are many in recent philosophy. Confronted with them several religious apologists have decided to settle for less than an absolute being. In some cases, as in many variations on the theme of a 'finite God', this being is still supernatural and far beyond the full understanding of our limited intellects. Others are content with a humanist God, a God who is not any kind of reality other than ourselves but some aspect of our own limited and finite experience, some slant we may have on the world, it may be, or some focus for our total experience or some moral ideal or policy to be sought after. This takes the sting out of the standard criticisms, but it is all the same a very short way with the opponent of religion or the sceptic. The religious person is not likely to be content for long with the attenuations of faith that leave no reality which can properly be worshipped, and the idea of a 'finite God', even when thought to be far above us in excellence and power, falls very far short of the worshipful reality which accounts for the serenity and peace which the truly religious person displays in the face of all untoward experience.

The solution which commends itself to the most perceptive defenders of religion lies in the renewal of the sense of the mystery and elusiveness of God of which the profoundest religious testimony speaks in such moving and impressive ways. We cannot hope to understand the way God has to be or comprehend what it means to be ultimate or absolute. Men do not know God in this way, and they never will. The mystery of the divine nature is irreducible, the 'essence of God', to use the traditional terms, cannot be discovered. But we find all the same that we have to recognize the inevitability of there being some reality which is transcendent or absolute in a way that passes all our comprehension. This is because finite being is incomplete in a way that calls for completion in some way that goes altogether beyond itself. Nothing finite fully explains itself. Explanation, as we normally provide it, is in terms of finite relations of various things to one another. This accounts for that, which in turn is due to something else, and so on. But this is a process that goes on *ad infinitum*, and as such it is essentially inadequate in a way that points to a reality beyond, which, from the nature of the case, is not to be comprehended in the same way.

There are many ways in which this sense of an infinite reality may be brought out. We may dwell upon the strangeness of anything being as it is at a particular time or of an actual present emerging out of what seems to be an infinite past. This makes it hard to avoid the conclusion that the order of things in a finite temporal way has some dependence on a reality altogether beyond the finite scheme of things and not, therefore, comprehensible in terms of the interrelations of things in a finite system. Or we may consider how inescapable we find it to seek some cause or explanation of all that happens. We account for this in terms of that and that in terms of something else, and so on. But there is no end to explanation in these terms and that again suggests that the ultimate accounting for things requires some order of being that is not limited in the same way and which does not therefore admit of being accounted for in turn. There are various poetic and religious ways in which the same awareness of a transcendent but essentially mysterious reality may be evoked.

This has been a recurrent theme in recent philosophy of religion, and I have no need to elaborate it at greater length here.[1] No one would claim that it is a novel theme, indeed much of its long history will be reflected in the matters to which I shall shortly proceed. But the need to meet the vigorous criticisms of empiricist and kindred writers has sharpened today the sense of the mystery and uniqueness which is involved in the inevitability of there being God. We have thus acquired considerable caution in speaking of God. Some have taken this to the length of not acknowledging that God is a reality at all. That is understandable

1. I have tried to present it carefully and with close reference to recent work in my *Teach Yourself: Philosophy of Religion*, E.U.P.

but also, it seems to me, altogether mistaken. If we like to say that the word 'existence' refers to entities or events in space and time we may do so, but this is very arbitrary linguistic legislation, and if we do adopt this odd way of talking, we have to be certain of compensating for it, as not all are careful to do, by making it clear that there is a genuine reference to talk about the transcendent and supreme being. Although thinkers have been tempted from time to time in the past to say that God is nothing, this must not be taken in any literal sense. Nor should it give any support to the supposition, so common in some quarters today, that the reference of religious utterance can be found entirely in a human or finite context, in particular features of present experience for example. The reference is to some reality altogether other than ourselves. But it is also understood more sharply than ever how elusive this reality is in itself and how impossible it is for us to characterize it directly or predicate anything about it in a quite explicit sense.

There arise in this way two very difficult problems. In the first place there is the problem of the ultimate relation of God to the world. Many have supposed that God as ultimate or absolute being must include all other reality in itself, and this has often been the dominant theme of much oriental thought. Others have argued that this form of absolutism or pantheism comes about from trying to bring within our own comprehension the elusive relation of God to the world which is essentially beyond the categories of our own thought. We try to rationalize matters which belong to the realm of the suprarational. This warning leaves it open to us to continue to insist on the genuinely finite nature of the finite facts we encounter in the world, including ourselves, and at the same time refer them, for their ultimate ground or condition, to a reality which is complete and self-contained and perfect as it is not possible for finite reality to be and which, for that reason, cannot be directly known or encountered. This is the attitude usually implied in western thought about God and in the emphasis on the relation of God to the world as absolute Lord or Creator, an emphasis by no means absent from oriental thought.

The second problem is that of the particular utterances made in religion and of the attitudes in which specific affirmations are at least implicit. How are these possible if the ultimate absolute being is as elusive as is contended, and how are they warranted? This is the basic form of the problem of religious symbolism. Some contend that no solution of this problem is possible and that silence is the only response we can properly make to the impact upon us of a supreme transcendent reality. Others have contended that there are various indirect ways in which the transcendent may be known from within present experience. How this is warranted is a very difficult question, and some have burked the question by appeals to authority, some more subtle than others. Recent religious thought has centred much on this question of the vindication of religious symbolism and the method of interpreting it. And however much the problem has been accentuated by the clear understanding that it is not a question of passing from one finite reality to another but of laying hold on a wholly transcendent reality at work within the world, the finer realization of the elusive and uniquely mysterious nature of the transcendent has enabled us to view the problem in a much clearer light. The solution may appear more baffling but we at least understand better what a solution requires.

With this goes a much subtler understanding of the problems of religion generally, and that carries within it a better appreciation of the points of resemblance and differences between religions. Many of the crudities involved in earlier studies of religion are thus avoided and the ground is prepared for a more profitable encounter of the religions of the world with one another. It is not a facile syncretism that is being sought but a genuinely new and sympathetic appreciation of one another's insights and points of difference. This is the true extension of an oecumenical spirit beyond the confines of particular religions today, and it is important that it should be conducted with understanding and patience as well as with enthusiasm. This is why we require, not merely fuller factual information about one another's religions, but a refinement of the understanding of what religious attitudes involve.

In an essay as short as the present one, I can only give a few sharp indications of the way the theme of the preceding passages is operative in the study of religions today. I shall begin with a reference to the way the sense of the transcendent appears in the earliest explicit records we have of the development of religious life and understanding, namely some of the sacred scriptures of India already noticed in Part One of this book.

IV

Of religious life in India before the first Dravidian invasions very little is known, and we have only very scanty knowledge of the early Dravidian period. There is some reason to believe that certain features of modern Hinduism owe something at least to the practices of these very early times. It appears, for example, that cattle were treated as sacred even then in the Indus valley where there is also evidence of a very ancient snake cult. The worship of the God Siva may well go back to this period; and the so-called 'animism' of some jungle tribes of today may have something to tell us even about the religion of prehistory in India. But whatever be the outcome of this and kindred speculations, I should be disposed to maintain that whatever religious practices may have preceded the great religions of India, the former would have been characterized, even in the most remote ages, by some impact on the rude minds of men of a transcendent reality, the sense of which would inform, in some degree and perhaps intermittently the customs we might otherwise describe as 'nature religion' or straightforward animism or polytheism. Confirmation of this seems to be forthcoming when we come to those stages of development at which we begin to have some reliable records.

This is the period which begins to see the birth of Vedic literature. These compositions, containing, it may be, man's first literary effort, 'the first word spoken by the Aryan Man' as it was put by Max Müller, must be associated mainly with the vigorous culture of the Nordic invaders who drifted into India early in the second millennium before Christ. They owe less to the Dravidian civilization or any primitive life on which these earlier invasions supervened. None the less there appears to have been much blending of the new religion and culture with the old, including the absorption of elements which may well have been indigenous; there is also the absence of any obvious signs of overt conflict at the religious level. It seems thus likely that the new religion, while developing and extending the old and making it more conscious of itself, would be taking up into its own life elements which, far from being alien or suited for absorption in purely external or formal ways, would be already in some regard modes of substantially the same experience. The blending could not be so complete or have taken the form it has if the new religion had meant something radically different from the old. The records of the new religion may thus reflect much that had been going on long before.

It must of course be admitted that the Nordics kept themselves apart when they could, and had much contempt for the peoples they conquered; but the view has also been advanced that the stirring of thought which gave us the Vedic writings was largely brought about by the inter-mingling of the invaders with the original inhabitants. The persistence of some features of the old religion in the new is, in any case, certain; and this it is that tempts us to conclude that the new religion in becoming articulate, without sharply dissociating itself from the old, would be giving expression to something incipient in the old religion also? May not the main difference even be that of greater selfcon-sciousness and clearer articulation? It would seem at any rate that enough has lived on from prehistory in Indian re-ligion to warrant the provisional assumption that there has been no radical discontinuity of essential nature between its dim beginnings and its higher and more reflective stages. It may thus be not too bold a speculation to regard the Vedic verses as some indication of the nature of religion in India long before these verses took shape themselves.

Even if there had been sharper conflict than any of which we have record between the religion of the Nordics and that of earlier inhabitants of the land they invaded, this would not wholly discredit the suggestion that has just been made. For the very articulation of religion may bring certain forms of it into opposition with others that sub-stantially resemble them, and many of the more incidental features of religion, those which root it in particular cus-toms and characteristics, may well be quite adequate occasions for conflict. But, in fact, the impression one seems to have of the early religion of India, is that at the religious level, the process of merging and integration of cultures was fairly consistent and natural, a fact that may be not without some connexion with the traditionally open and all-embracing tendencies of later Hinduism. The significance of the Vedic writings as clues to problems about the origin of religion may thus be more extensive in range than might be warranted by too close an association of them with one feature only of early Indian history.

In any case we must not forget the very great age of the Vedic writings themselves, especially when we allow for the fact that many of them were transmitted from one generation to the other orally long before they were committed to writing – as happened also to other religious documents of great importance at later times in India. They take us back to a very early period in the history of civilization and have much to tell us about the first stages of transition from primitive life to the beginnings of culture. The fact that they are the earliest Aryan documents would not of itself establish their claim to be closest to the primitive, for the obvious reason that man has not left the primitive stage at the same time or in quite the same way in all parts of the world. There are still very backward peoples in being. But we are not likely to see the latter in any normal process of emergence to more cultured existence, since any progress they make today will be certain to be that brought about by the sharp impact of modern civilization upon them. Our records of the Vedic age, on the other hand, put us at a point of peculiar advantage to note the affinity between an early culture and ruder modes of existence from which it emerged. This gives them distinctive importance for sociology in general, but what concerns us strictly now is what we can learn from them about the beginnings of religion.

Two points only will be made here. The first is that some of the earliest Vedic hymns, namely those contained in the *Rig Veda*, have a poetic beauty and numinous quality, even in transcription, which awakens in us, as they presumably stirred in their composers and original reciters, a reaction similar to the experience of God made possible for us normally by other means today. If we apply the test which I have defended elsewhere of regarding these early media of religious life from within our own religious consciousness, the reference away to a transcendent reality seems unmistakable. But if this consideration appears to depend too much on the position which it is intended to support, let us look at other features of these early Vedas.

Perhaps I may record first the general impression of these writings provided by Professor S. Radhakrishnan. He is eminently well qualified, both by his knowledge of his own religion and by his familiarity with modern thought, to give an instructive opinion, and he writes –

The *Rig Veda* which comprises 1,017 hymns divided into ten books, represents the earliest phase in the evolution of religious consciousness where we have not so much the commandments of priests as the outpourings of poetic minds who were struck by the immensity of the universe and the inexhaustible mystery of life. The reactions of simple yet unsophisticated minds to the wonder of existence are portrayed in these joyous hymns which attribute divinity to the striking aspects of nature.[1]

This hints at more than mere animism or straightforward polytheism. The 'wonder of existence' is that which has always been felt in religion. But closer investigation will carry us further. For there appear in the Vedic Pantheon certain divinities which stand in a peculiar relation to the others, in that they tend to reduce other deities to limited manifestations of themselves. Dy-aus, the Creator, and Varuna are 'high Gods' of this kind, Varuna in particular being regarded as a moral ruler of the world rewarding virtue and punishing sins. Nor is it altogether sound to regard these 'high Gods' as signs of the first beginnings of ethical monotheism. They certainly do represent an advance upon a more polytheistic stage, but they do more than that, the position being much more complicated than the gradual abandonment of polytheism for some form of monistic religion.

1. *The Principal Upanisads*, p. 30.

The clue to the true position may, I think, again be found in the words of Radhakrishnan when he speaks of the tendency

> when worship is accorded to any of the Vedic deities ... to make that deity the supreme one, of whom all others are forms or manifestations. He is given all the attributes of a monotheistic deity. As several deities are exalted to the first place, we get what has been called henotheism, as distinct from monotheism. There is, of course, a difference between a psychological monotheism where one God fills the entire life of the worshipper and a metaphysical monotheism. Synthesizing processes, classification of gods, simplification of the ideas of divine attributes and powers prepare for a metaphysical unity, the one principle informing all deities.[1]

The point to note especially here is that it seems possible, at a certain stage of development, to regard more than one deity as supreme, as almost the one sole God. This may seem to us flatly contradictory and a position in which it would not be possible for any mind to find lodgement at all. But we also know enough today of some of the extraordinary ways in which our minds do work on occasion, even at our stage of intellectual development, to find it not beyond comprehension that, just as early thinkers seem to have believed in a coexistence of opposites, so it was possible for a colourful polytheistic religion to have also a distinctively monistic aspect.

The conclusion to which this points is, in my opinion, that we should not regard monotheism as a completely new departure in religion, but as the bringing into consciousness, not always in the most adequate forms, of what has been latent from the start. How far this new understanding was the achievement of particular peoples, how and when they communicated it to others, are matters outside the scope of this inquiry. It will suffice for us to note the

1. op. cit., p. 33.

presence, prior to any intellectual monism, of intimations of an underlying unity of religious experience in the form of some sense of one supreme reality animating various forms of worship not overtly or consistently monistic. If this could be true at the level at which we hear of Gods like Varuna or Brahman, may it not also present us with the true way of regarding polytheism and animism in yet simpler and less reflective forms. I venture to think that it is along lines like these that we should tackle the problems of the history and comparative study of early religions, being careful not to be misled by too sharp an antithesis of polytheism and monism or the expectation that the monistic alternative to polytheism should always have the form of the monotheism with which we are acquainted ourselves.

Of particular interest here also is the early manifestation in the Vedic writings of the cautious religious scepticism which, as discerning writers have much stressed of late, is very far from profound faith. I turn to Radhakrishnan again for striking examples: 'it is said of Indra: "Of whom they ask, where is He! Of him indeed they also say, he is not." In another remarkable hymn, the priests are invited to offer a song of praise to Indra, "a true one, if in truth he is, for many say, there is no Indra, who has ever seen him? To whom are we to direct this song of praise?" . . . In another hymn Prajapati is praised as the creator and preserver of the world and as the one god, but the refrain occurs in verse after verse "what god shall we honour by means of sacrifice?"'[1] If words of this sort appear in a religion which is largely polytheistic, the impression is deepened that polytheism always contained within itself, and was perhaps made possible, by a latent monism. The idea of a supreme reality which is 'not this, not that', a refrain so common in subsequent religious literature, seems to go very far back

1. op. cit., p. 34.

and to confirm, in that way, the view that men have had from very early times some intimations of a divine existence which is present in all things but which it is risky to characterize in any particular way. The more explicit formulations of this conviction may have tended towards pantheism more than any other view, and many later developments of them may be too pantheistic to our taste. But this is understandable; if 'The Beyond' is also in all things, it might easily come to be identified, in attempts to refer expressly to it, with 'all things'. But I also much incline to the view that, with the keener appreciation we have today of what the transcendent character of God implies, we may find reason to doubt the strictly pantheistic nature of much that used to be regarded as such and to look behind seemingly pantheistic formulations of religion, and any ill-effect these may have had on subsequent religious developments, to the caution which points to the authentic character of an awareness of the transcendent. It seems therefore that, if the view can be maintained that the early Vedic documents reflect much on a wide range which went on long before their actual composition in the form in which they were recorded, we have substantial confirmation in this source for the view that some consciousness of the transcendent is a more pervasive feature of the practices in which religion as we know it began than used to be supposed.

V

The conclusion at which we arrived in the previous section can be reinforced if the *Upanisads*, for which the earlier Vedic hymns and priestly writings prepared the way, can in turn be regarded as bringing to more articulate expression much which had been germinating for a long time before them. It does not follow that that is all they did.

But if it is safe to assume the sort of continuity I have suggested, and the anticipation of the teaching of the *Upanisads* in such aspects of earlier Vedic writings as those already indicated seems to warrant that, the *Upanisads* are peculiarly revealing documents for the study of the centuries which preceded them. Some support for this view may also be found in a further more indirect way which may be worth noting here.

This turns on the close similarity between the main doctrines of the *Upanisads* and the speculations of some of the more notable Greek philosophers, including Plato. The parallel between the teaching of Plato, especially where the control of appetite and the conquest of ignorance by some supreme illumination of the soul is concerned, and the main features of Indian thought still awaits careful scholarly investigation; when undertaken, I submit, it will be very rewarding. At the moment, however, I wish only to mention an explanation often given of the similarities between the *Upanisads* and Greek philosophy. It is that both these have elements that go back to a common origin. In offering this explanation, allowance must be made for some measure of interaction between Greece and India in the classical period of Greek civilization. The Pythagoreans and Plato certainly knew something about Indian thought and there is reason to believe that Plato had some contact with an Indian philosopher who visited Athens about the time the *Parmenides* was composed. But on the whole contacts of this kind were scanty, and it seems more plausible to ascribe the similarities between Greek and Indian philosophy to a common origin, unless, of course, we can regard them as wholly fortuitous. That they were quite fortuitous seems to me very unlikely, since they manifest themselves in early stages of development as well as in the final product. But if we are to postulate some ferment of thought in the East to which Greece and

India alike are indebted (as they seem certainly indebted to a common source for their languages) we must place it a very long time before the composition of the *Upanisads* in the eighth and seventh centuries B.C. That links the *Upanisads* with a process of development over a long time which would undoubtedly be religious in character.

But whatever we make of this particular argument, it is certain that the *Upanisads* themselves provide a remarkable example of speculative thinking, connected closely and at an early date with the practice of religion, which gives us ideas of God's transcendence closely similar to much that we find in theology and the philosophy of religion today. The main theme of the *Upanisads* is that the world is not self-caused or self-maintaining. Its existence presupposes a more ultimate or absolute 'first principle'. There is thus one supreme reality behind and beyond the flux of the world. This is unknowable and incomprehensible. How the 'One' is related to 'the many' in the flux of change is a further question about which more than one view may be found in the *Upanisads* and in the work of later writers which they inspired. Sometimes, but not very often, we are left with the impression that the finite world is being treated as a mere illusion or an evil dream out of which we must do our best to wake up. But as a rule the *Upanisads* betray an acuter consciousness than this of the problem of the 'appearances' and their status. They speak, for example, of the finite as a self-limitation of the infinite. In other contexts we read of creation as a self-expression or projection of 'the Supreme'. This in turn gives place elsewhere to ideas more closely resembling the Christian doctrine of creation. The world exists by the free choice of the One, it is sustained by 'the play' of God. The sense in which God could be said to be personal as well as superpersonal is sometimes considered, and the eternal is frequently taken to be at the same time immanent in the world. The transcendent which is 'wholly other', in the modern phrase, yet enters into the life of man and lives in him. The infinite dwelling in the finite and the individual which is thus also infinite, one with all cosmic existence, gives the idea also of the One Universal Self which is the true self of each individual. To realize this true self through which we are identical with the eternal becomes thus the aim of religious contemplation, intellectual inquiry and moral discipline. It requires rigorous intellectual discipline and exacting moral self-control. This, in spite of its severity, is not altogether world-denying or always uncompromisingly ascetic. For even the futilities of human life are material for the unfolding of the Divine which dwells in all things. It is detachment and not indifference that has to be cultivated, and this is consistent with high respect for the transient realities of the world and even for the continuance in the world, for the sake of the world, of those who have received the final illumination of their identity with the Eternal Self within them. Hence the insistence on social service, on compassion, virtue, welfare, as well as on study and teaching. But however the relation of the finite self to the Eternal Self is conceived, and whatever variations of emphasis we may find in the account given of the relation of the one to the other and of degrees of reality (sometimes with corresponding degrees of worth closely resembling the same notion in modern idealism) accorded to finite things, the transcendent character of the absolute reality is always very clearly understood in a way that not only lends special interest to these early anticipations of later attempts to conceive the relation of the finite to the infinite, but which also proves exceptionally instructive to those who wish to consider the problem of transcendence as it presents itself today.

The affinity between the teaching of the *Upanisads* and the main contentions of the so-called 'Continental Theologians' of today who have brought the idea of transcendence into prominence and given us a renewed appreciation of its absolute character, has been admirably brought out by a noted student of eastern thought, W. S. Urquhart.[1] He has also indicated the points at which the absolutism of the Vedantic writers, in the sense of the identification of the finite with the indwelling transcendent reality, would be unacceptable to theologians like Barth and Brunner, and has in fact been denounced by them. But there remains a task that is perhaps yet more important and interesting, and one which it is to be hoped a competent scholar will soon undertake, the task namely of delineating the striking affinities which subsist between some of the most incisive doctrines of these Indian scriptures, still imperfectly known in the West, and those growing points of modern philosophy where the main lessons of recent empiricism are giving us a clearer insight into the nature of speculative questions. What positivism and rigorous empiricism have to teach the religious thinker – and we have seen that indirectly they have a great deal to teach him today notwithstanding much initial incompatibility of aim and sympathy – lies very close to some of the most suggestive teaching of the *Upanisads* and their methods.

A text which has undertones strongly suggestive of very familiar notes in recent thought is one of which we have no record in any extant *Upanisad*, but which is mentioned by the later commentator and religious thinker Sankara. It tells of a pupil who pleads with his teacher to expound to him the nature of the Absolute Self understood religiously as Brahman. To each request the teacher turns a deaf ear until at last he answers the insistent 'Teach me, sir', with the words: 'I am teaching you but you do not follow. The Self is silence.' Echoes of more traditional variations on the theme of the *via negativa* are also frequent.

1. *Humanism and Christianity*, Ch. VI.

Absolute being is held not to be a quality of things, but to be almost opposed to things; but, if it is in this way 'non-being' or 'nothingness', that is only because its reality is such as to elude predication. No logical derivation of it is possible, although intellectual knowledge has its place in the process by which the intuition of Supreme Being is possible. It is also maintained that although the Absolute cannot be described discursively, it is possible for the seer to translate his vision into significant terms through hints and images and symbols – we might compare the 'slant-wise' communication of which Evelyn Underhill speaks. In this process both human effort and Divine grace are at work, and in the unveiling or self-disclosure of 'the Real' to us there is also a concealment; if this is not understood in quite the same way as Brunner's 'mystery mysteriously revealed', the points of similarity are none the less striking. Equally suggestive of a theme familiar in recent transcendentalist theology, but again understood in ways that have affinity also with absolute idealism, is the denial of the applicability of the distinction of subject and object to Supreme Being. Of the richness and originality and incisiveness with which many of these strikingly modern themes are handled in the *Upanisads*, and of the help the study of the latter may be to us, this is not the place to speak in detail. But I hope I have given some indication of the insight into the nature of the transcendent, and into the way we must approach it in thought, which is to be found in these very ancient religious documents.

It has also to be stressed that, although the *Upanisads* can properly be regarded as philosophical in nature, or at least as containing much that is so and that of rare quality, they are also essentially the products of profound religious vision. To use the words of Radhakrishnan:

As a part of the Veda, the *Upanisads* belong to *sruti* or revealed literature. They are immemorial, *sanatana*, timeless.

Their truths are said to be breathed out by God or visioned by the seers. They are the utterances of the sages who speak out of the fullness of their illumined experience. They are not reached by ordinary perception, inference or reflection, but *seen* by the seers, even as we see and not infer the wealth and riot of colour in the summer sky. The seers have the same sense of assurance and possession of their spiritual vision as we have of our physical perception. . . . Symbolically, the *Upanisads* describe revelation as the breath of God blowing on us . . . (they) are vehicles more of spiritual illumination than of systematic reflection.[1]

Finally, the authors of the *Upanisads* are deeply conscious of their indebtedness to others, and often quote texts from the early Vedas in support of their teaching, much as the composers of the *Rig Veda* in turn tell us of 'the ancient makers of the path'. There is a continuity of development, and a transition by almost imperceptible gradations, from the earlier Vedas through the priestly *Brahmanas* and the mystic *Aranyakas* to the more philosophical *Upanisads*. The latter bring out what is implicit in the Vedic hymns and provide a more express solution to the problems posed by these hymns than they ventured to offer themselves. The notable 'Hymn of Creation' is an unusually striking example of the anticipation of the ripest teaching of the *Upanisads*:

It seeks to explain the universe as evolving out of One. But the One is no longer a god like Indra or Varuna, Praja-pati or Visvakarman. The hymn declares that all these gods are of late or of secondary origin. They know nothing of the beginning of things. The first principle, that one, *tad ekam,* is uncharacterizable. It is without qualities or attributes, even negative ones. To apply to it any description is to limit and bind that which is limitless and boundless. 'That one breathed breathless. There was nothing else.'[2]

1. *The Principal Upanisads*, pp. 22 and 23.
2. op. cit., p. 35.

What we find in fact very often is that Vedic writers were themselves led to think of the Vedic deities 'as different names of the One Universal Godhead, each representing some essential power of the divine being. . . . They express different qualities of the object worshipped'.[1] By reinterpretation the pluralistic elements of the earlier writings come to be held together more firmly in the *Upanisads* as multiform aspects of one supreme religious reality.

Here again, therefore, we seem to find support for the view that the *Upanisads* must be regarded as the culmination of a long process of religious development, one which was becoming increasingly conscious of itself, in which the final achievement is the ripening of what was imperfectly and less reflectively present in men's religious experience long before. This process of development is a complicated one, and there is certainly more involved in it than the emergence into more explicit consciousness of what had previously been only very vaguely apprehended. But all that I wish to suggest at the moment is that the relation between the *Upanisads* themselves and the religious life of the preceding centuries, as reflected especially in anticipations of the *Upanisads* in earlier religious compositions, affords us reasons additional to those already noted for supposing that some apprehension of a transcendent reality, and the worship thereof, has always been a factor in the main development of religious life in India.

VI

The importance of a due understanding of the nature of the transcendent, and of its peculiar sort of elusiveness and mystery, can be brought out further if we turn now to a different problem that presents itself in the study of eastern religions, namely the question whether we should think of Buddhism as a religion involving a worship of God. As

1. op. cit., p. 40.

will be evident from what has been said in Part One of this book, there is a case for regarding some of the stricter and earlier forms of Buddhism as a 'religion without God'. This may seem a paradoxical situation to many western students, but it will be claimed by many adherents to the Buddhist religion themselves, as well as by outside observers, that one form of Buddhism at least is atheistic. This seems to me however not the final truth of the matter, and I think it is very instructive to consider both what makes it plausible to say that Buddhism, in some forms, is a religion without God and why this is also misleading in the final analysis. I propose therefore, at this point, to look again at this feature of Buddhism and consider in illustration of my main theme, how it should be understood in the light of recent religious thought. One of the main sources of the atheistic interpretation of Buddhism is the *Pali Canon*, and I shall have that in mind especially in the observations that follow.

Let me begin with the facts about Buddha which seem to be beyond reasonable dispute and which most, though by no means all, scholars would accept. For these we rely mostly on the *Pali Canon*. This collection of sacred texts was not committed to writing till late in the first century B.C. But there is every reason to suppose that it had been substantially assembled long before that time, preservation being ensured by an elaborate and highly skilful method of oral transmission. The main period for the composition of these texts appears to have been between 500 and 250 B.C., the *Canon* being closed according to a strong tradition in the reign of King Asoka whose influence on the development of Buddhism was particularly extensive. The dating of the texts within the period just specified is not so easy, although there seem to be reasonable grounds for singling out some parts of the *Canon* as being earlier, and presumably more authentic, than others. The connexion between the texts in question and the alleged occurrence of certain Buddhist Councils, one of them being placed very soon after the death of Buddha, has been a very fertile source of disputation which does not seem to have produced any particularly helpful results so far as the understanding of the main claims of Buddhism is concerned. The points of most importance which do emerge for us are these.

There is nothing in Buddhism strictly analogous to the Christian Kerygma, partly because of the different circumstances in which the message of Buddha began to be propagated, and partly because of differences in the content of what is offered. The peculiar significance ascribed by Christians to certain historical events has no parallel in Buddhism, and Buddha himself, according to the famous text which described his disease, disavowed at the time of his death any peculiar claims to be made on his behalf as the instrument of salvation. It was the doctrine that he bequeathed to others and it was the doctrine that really mattered, although this advice was extensively disregarded. But while the early followers of Buddha had thus not the same motive as the first Christians for cherishing the memory of the founder and preserving intact the available reports about him, veneration for Buddha himself appears, from the internal evidence of the sacred texts themselves and the mode of their preservation, to have been very profound among his first disciples, and it seems very certain that the *Pali Canon* contains substantially the beliefs about Buddha and his teaching held by his close contemporaries and immediate successors, and thus, presumably, the views of Buddha himself. If there is error we have certainly no good independent source from which to correct it, and the attempt to discriminate within the *Canon* itself on *a priori* grounds has no clear principle on which we could justify the exclusion of any substantial part of the content of the *Canon*.

In the light of this it seems reasonable to believe certain things about the historical Buddha. He was born of noble and prosperous parents and brought up in happy and comfortable circumstances. But in due course – according to legend at an early age – he began to be depressed by the thought of decay, disease, and death. The transitory nature of all earthly pleasures brought him a sense of deep frustration. In consequence of this he left his home to become a wandering seeker after truth, hoping in this way to attain a higher life which would put him out of reach of the ills which preyed on his mind. There were many such wanderers and recluses at the time in his country seeking some sort of release from the ills and frustrations of the present existence by completer union with a supreme reality, the 'One', beyond the flux of change. The close relation between such practices and the teaching of the *Upanisads* and the general religious culture which these reflect, is evident. Buddha began as others began in his day, and we must not lose sight of this in our final account of his teaching.

The first practices to which Buddha turned were the prevalent Yoga or Jhana methods of meditation, but these only brought him to a state of mental vacuum which was little relieved by sustained experiments with other methods of psychological spiritual training. He therefore intensified his efforts by endeavouring to eliminate bodily hindrances to meditation yet more completely in the course of an exceptionally severe asceticism. 'Because I ate so little', he is reported as saying, 'my members . . . grew like the knotted joints of withered creepers', his gaunt ribs were 'like crazy rafters' and at one stage he decided to dispense with food altogether. The intensity of these ascetic practices won the admiration of other wandering seekers who seemed convinced that some overwhelming triumph must result from such unmitigated austerity. But this also proved unavailing, and Buddha appears to have become convinced that ruthless mortification of the body was no stage on the way to his goal. Not long after this discovery and the consequent abandonment of his extreme asceticism, there happened to Buddha the special experience from which the religion he founded properly takes its start, an experience of 'enlightenment' from which is derived the name Buddha, 'the Enlightened One'.

This experience brought to Buddha an understanding, so he claimed, of a chain of causes which brought about decay and suffering. The first link in this chain is ignorance, but this is also the link that is broken by the sort of understanding which Buddha himself achieved. To reach a similar state of release there is required much intellectual and moral discipline. The extremes of asceticism and sensuality are to be avoided, the celebrated Middle Path being also described as the Eightfold Path involving 'right views, right purpose, right speech, right conduct, right livelihood, right endeavour, right mindfulness, right concentration'. It is not to our purpose to consider these principles in detail, but it can easily be understood how Buddhism became a highly ethical religion, although, as with other religions, practice did not always conform with intention. The virtues which Buddha extolled, and of which he managed to gain extraordinary practitioners, are certainly noble virtues. Cruelty, dishonesty, theft and unchastity come under severe censure, but avoidance of such views is by no means a merely legalistic or negative achievement; it is bound up with the positive qualities of loving-kindness, compassion, gladness, and equanimity. Buddha himself has been described as 'a good diner-out with a fund of anecdote'. The detachment which his disciples are to cultivate is not indifference or formal correctness, it involves positive regard for others and a noble unselfishness to which Buddhism owes much of its greatness and its influence for good where it has not been debased.

This emphasis on mental and moral excellence is in some measure responsible for the impression that Buddhism is an atheistic religion, the suggestion being sometimes made that Buddha turned away from the other-worldly pre-occupations of his contemporaries and the arid, if not revolting, asceticism which went with it, to a healthy and balanced regard for human well-being in all its forms. In substance, his teaching involved the restoration of human values and human dignity, and it has thus to be regarded, so some maintain, as a reaction from the traditional trans-cendentalism and a protest in the name of human worth. But this view, as it stands, will bear little examination.

This is because the practice of the virtues instanced above is regarded by Buddha and his followers as part of the process of attaining liberation through the dispelling of ignorance, the virtues being regarded as the natural result of release and illumination quite as much as they are held to be preconditions of it . To regard Buddhism as a plea for the restoration of moral values and other human excellences to a place of supreme importance, in neglect of the special teaching about ignorance as a link in the chain of causes that leads to temporal ills, is, in truth, to omit what seems on all the evidence the kernel of the teaching of Buddha himself and of Buddhist doctrine as perpetuated after-wards. The ethical teaching of Buddha is indissolubly connected with the notion of liberation through the illumi-nation that overcomes ignorance. We have therefore to consider more carefully what is involved in this particular crucial feature of Buddhist belief and how far it also admits of a secular or humanistic interpretation.

VII

It is just here that the case for the atheistic interpretation of Buddha seems strongest. For when the question: 'What

does Buddha specifically say about the experience of enlightenment, what views does he advance which could be
regarded as some sort of pronouncement about God in the
proper sense of the term, what does he say about the 'beyond' or about some other reality than the world as we
normally experience it?' – When all this is raised we have
no answer to offer that is not entirely negative. Buddha
appears to have studiously avoided any sort of pronouncement that could in any way be regarded as an answer to
questions such as those listed; he has done this deliberately
and not through oversight or preoccupation with other
matters. The advice he gave to his followers also is to
avoid metaphysical or religious speculation. A form of
Socratic technique is used in exposition of the essential doctrines, but this is not to be extended to matters which fall
outside the strict doctrine. All speculation about other
'ultimate' questions is a useless and even misleading
diversion of energy.

There fall under condemnation in this way many of the
philosophical inquiries which had been of most concern to
the writers of the *Upanisads* and on which the subtleties of
their thought had been most ingeniously expended. We
have on record[1] a list of not less than sixty-two questions
which are thought thus to go beyond the limits of legitimate
inquiry. They include the questions whether the soul or the
world is eternal, whether the soul survives the dissolution
of the body and whether its consciousness, if the soul
retains consciousness after death, is limited or not, together
with many questions about form and formlessness,
finite and infinite, the caused or fortuitous origin of the
world, and the status of beings who were once gods in
heaven but have for some reason or another fallen from
their high state. The probability is that questions of this
kind were much canvassed at various times by some Budd-

1. In the *Brahmajäla Sutta*.

hists, sometimes with an exasperating abuse of ingenuity. But the more orthodox attitude was firmly to discourage such questions; and while this was possibly due in part to understandable impatience with misguided subtlety, it seems certain also that Buddha himself set his face resolutely against intellectual efforts designed to find some solution to the problems in question or others like them. His attitude to all such matters, and the attitude enjoined on his followers, seems to have been one of resolute silence.

Taken along with the denial of a substantival self in a way which to us today brings Hume much to mind, notwithstanding that there is some important sense in which the soul persists for some period at least in Buddhist teaching, this uncompromising silence of Buddha on all matters outside his 'doctrine' may easily be taken as requiring the atheistic interpretation of his view whereby the 'release' of which he spoke had reference to nothing beyond man himself. It was a state to be attained by our own efforts, and even if it went beyond anything we normally encountered, it involved nothing beyond the agent himself. Man finds his salvation in himself and for himself, there is no divine intervention, no mediation, no sublime object of worship outside of man himself. This is how the negative side of Buddha's teaching is often understood. None the less it seems to me that there are weighty considerations which we can put into the other side of the scale.

In the first place, it seems to be entirely unplausible to hold, as many have done, that the famous 'release' meant no more for Buddha than complete annihilation. Longing and pain are over, on the view sometimes ascribed to Buddha, because everything is over. We find peace only when we totally cease to exist. This seems to me certainly mistaken. Admittedly 'nirvana', the state which the enlightened attain, does mean a state of being 'blown out', as a candle is blown out. But scholars would agree that the idea of extinction in the physical sense, as when a fire is extinguished would not have meant utter annihilation to Buddha's contemporaries; it would have meant return to some more pure invisible state. To the extent that the comparison with fire appears, as it does more than once, in the main Buddhist records, this seems to confirm the view that something more positive than literal extinction is meant by 'release' and 'enlightenment' in Buddhist teaching. We may also argue that, if sheer annihilation were the end, the Buddhist 'Way' would have no particular relevance. I shall indeed be stressing in a moment that the connexion between the moral and intellectual practices commended by Buddha and the state to be finally attained is not a straightforward rational one such as we would ordinarily establish between certain ends and the activities by which these are attained, and there might thus seem to be no special reason why the Buddhist 'Way' should not be regarded as a condition of annihilation as of anything else. But I think we are entitled to presuppose some suitability, and it appears to me highly unlikely that a sage whose insight is at certain levels at least beyond question could have thought the elaborate disciplines he describes to be bound up with the attainment of a totally negative state of extinction. 'Enlightenment' certainly does mean the 'blowing out' of certain things, including desire and concern for one's own attainment. The attitude of the released one is that of perfect detachment. Finite life as we know it comes also to an end, there is no further rebirth. But this does not preclude there being some kind of positive significance attaching to the state of release or 'nirvana'. Nor is it likely that the mere expectation of release in the sense of annihilation, even if much to be desired in the light of the pain and frustration thought to be our destiny in finite life, would have elicited such warmth and depth of enthusiasm and such overwhelming joy as that displayed by the early Buddhist saints. Many scholars also maintain that 'nirvana', although most frequently defined in negative terms, is sometimes referred to in unmistakably positive language. The words for 'immortal' (*amata pada*) and 'perpetual' (*accanta*) are apparently to be understood in that way. It seems thus that we must accept the view, commended by most scholars today, that 'release' has some positive import in Buddhist teaching.

The second point which needs to be emphasized here is that the ignorance which Buddha wishes to overcome is no ordinary ignorance to be dispelled in a normal way. It is not as if Buddha had discovered some new facts about the world or about ourselves in the way the scientist or the philosopher usually come by their views. There is indeed a close connexion, which all can appreciate, between motives of which we are not always conscious, especially subtle forms of selfishness, and the ills to which we are heir. Social disorders can be traced in part to this source as well as many personal ills, such as the anxiety neuroses which seem so prevalent at present and which bring in their turn many physical ailments. To understand this is at least one way to peace and the conquest of evil, and Buddha must have reflected much on such matters, in a way that accords him peculiar interest for the psychologist of today, during the long period of intense meditation which preceded his enlightenment; this no doubt enters into his teaching about detachment and the serenity which comes by it. But the peculiar claim which Buddha puts forward seems plainly to go far beyond any psychological or philosophical wisdom of this sort. If, for example, the objection were made that not all evils could be traced to the sources mentioned, one would feel that the objection was not really relevant, that what Buddha taught was on an entirely different plane, or in a quite different frame of reference, from that where argument and counter argument have place. For good or ill he was claiming a very special insight into very special matters.

This becomes plainer when we consider the way Buddha's doctrine is to be commended to others. The process certainly involves teaching and rational exposition, but there is no question of putting all intelligent and earnest seekers straightway in possession of the truth. To over-come the ignorance which lies at the root of evil is essen-tially a matter of undergoing a certain experience or attaining to a certain state; and that is just how release came to Buddha himself in the first instance.

It is worth noting carefully the immediate antecedents of the actual 'enlightenment'. Buddha appears to have had intimations himself of the approach of a signal event in his life connected with his abandonment of strict asceticism. He recalled, for example, an experience of ecstasy he had in his youth under a tree on his father's land, he felt himself purified and cleansed within, made firm and inwardly aloof but not cut away altogether from his surroundings; and in this specially elevated frame of mind he came to 'a delight-ful spot with goodly groves and a clear flowing river'. Here, according to the traditional account, he determined to *wait* till the enlightenment came. He passed through many experiences serving as the preparation for high states, most of them having analogues in the meditative practices of his time, until he finally reached the rapturous condition in which he had complete assurance that he had been delivered finally from the process of becoming and rebirth. In this condition there came to him also the 'form-ula' which leads from the fact of suffering to its cessation.

For an adequate account of Buddha's experience and of the records and sources from which the account must be constructed, the reader must go elsewhere. Nor is this the place to institute comparison with other recorded states of similar rapture, or to consider what light the psychologist can throw on such experiences. But it needs no detailed or vivid picture to make it altogether plain that the illumination which Buddha claimed, although its substance can be partly set out and taught as a system, falls into an entirely different class from the normal discovery of truth at the scientific or philosophical level. It has more in common with the raptures of the artist. This does not mean that inspiration in science or philosophy has nothing in common with inspiration in art or religion. As a rule we find in both cases a long period of groping, perhaps with no evident advance, followed by a sudden illumination, of the approach of which there may or may not be intimations beforehand. There are no doubt other important resemblances. Yet no one can question the differences, including especially the ability of the scientist or philosopher to communicate fairly directly, as a rule, to suitably qualified persons, and perhaps to the layman, the substance of what he has learnt. The artist cannot do this. But we must not press the analogy with art too closely here. For the point to be noted most of all is that Buddha is claiming an insight of a quite peculiar kind which it does not normally fall to the lot of human beings to acquire in any measure. Buddha sitting under his tree is thus a very different figure from Descartes sitting by his stove; Buddha's waiting is a very special waiting, and the claim he eventually advances is meant to be put to the proof in a very special way by those who are themselves able to enter into similar rapturous states to his own and receive thereby the peculiar assurances which are reserved for 'the enlightened'; and we certainly pass beyond ordinary secularism or humanism here.

There are also, in the third place, some further, more specific claims which it seems certain that Buddha himself made about his experience, notably that it gave him, on the one hand, the sight of other beings passing hence and reappearing in other births, and, on the other, the assurance that he himself had been finally freed from the chain of rebirths. Along with this knowledge would go also the ability to know other people's minds in some supernormal way and the awareness that he himself could prolong his present temporal existence for a fabulous period, notwithstanding that he had already entered the state of enlightenment. Connected with this in turn, and possibly accepted by Buddha himself as well as his followers, is the belief that extraordinary conditions attended the birth of Buddha and of others who fulfilled a similar role to his in other ages, before or after him. Buddha is also thought to be superior to various deities, it is they who make obeisance to him, and he himself is quoted as denying that he is one of the gods on the ground of his superiority to them, an attitude he does not scruple to adopt apparently even towards the highest of the gods, *Brahma*. The adversaries who tempt him are more than human, the demon of the eclipse is cowed by him, and his own colour is transfigured at the moment he receives supreme insight. The attainment of *nirvana* confers on other saints also supernormal powers.

Detailed exemplification of these claims would be out of place here. All that we need to note is the abundance of evidence that Buddha and other Buddhist saints were credited with, and presumably claimed themselves, extraordinary insights and supernatural powers such as those listed and similar in many regards to the claims we find in other religions. Now this in itself is far from proving that Buddhism contained a belief in God or some consciousness of Him, as the term 'God' is normally used today, least of all if God is regarded as a transcendent being. For 'supernatural' powers, in the sense of the instances alleged, although they take us far beyond anything we normally expect of human beings, and perhaps beyond anything we consider possible for a 'mere human', do not give us more than extraordinary superhuman powers and beings vastly superior to man, not divine power and God. But I do not think we can leave even this matter just where it stands. For I myself would find it hard, for the reasons set out in my discussion of paganism elsewhere,[1] to account for beliefs in the powers and phenomena in question in any final way, however unplausible we may consider these beliefs at their face value, except as the reflection at some point of truly numinous experiences of the transcendent.

But the crucial point where this consideration combines with the other observations I have made into a fairly firm conclusion seems to me to be found by going back to the matters which seemed at first to present the most formidable obstacle to any assimilation of Buddhism to the worship of a transcendent God, namely the persistent and deliberate silence of Buddha. It seems to me impossible to regard this as the bare agnosticism of the baffled or the disillusioned philosopher. It is the attitude of a visionary, the stillness of thought when it goes beyond itself and is impatient with itself; and the very fact that it is in connexion with our knowledge of the transcendent that our thought reaches most obviously and finally this limit which reduces it to negations, however much these may need to be supplemented in other ways of which not every religious visionary has taken due heed, convinces me that the argument which might seem to be the strongest in the armoury of those who give an atheistic account of Buddha can cut in precisely the opposite direction to that in which it is commonly taken. That Buddha himself may not always have appreciated what his attitude involved may readily be admitted. His negation may even have appeared to him to be bare negation, although I very much doubt it, but that does not preclude its having a positive

1. *Our Experience of God*, Chs. III and IV.

significance in the experience which it reflects and of which the literal terms of the overt description may not always be the fullest or most accurate indication. A very sound instinct may have led Buddha to suspect that an attempt to lay hold on a visionary experience in rational terms dispels it or diverts attention to other matters.

There is in fact one well-known and very significant section of the *Pali Canon* where Buddha seems to be expressly dissociating himself from the rational agnostic or any formal agnosticism. He will not have it that we can speculate even to the extent of formally expressing an agnostic position. We are not to say that we can say nothing; and this seems to me to give agnosticism a twist which completely alters its character and brings it into line with the acknowledgement of an ultimate mystery, a mystery whose ultimate and positive nature is discerned in a peculiarly incisive and modern way in this particular instance of Buddha's refusal to sanction open agnosticism.

I should attach much importance also to a circumstance of Buddha's own 'enlightenment' which is not generally thought to be especially revealing, namely the toning of it by his immediate environment and the cognizance he took of pleasing aspects of nature as integrated into the experience as a whole. In other cases, perhaps we should say in other cultures, we read of 'a burning bush', of the voice of God starkly out of the whirlwind or the storm, or at least a still small voice. Not so here, but the immediate environment has still its gentle part to play and one which is no less instructive to the student of today because it is subdued and elusive. It appears to me that it is in a peculiarly intimate fusion with present experience, not mainly or invariably physical, that knowledge of God is mediated to us. At the moment it must suffice to draw attention to the somewhat neglected inter-connexion of Buddha's natural environment and his experience at the climax of his career as further indication of the latter's conforming to the type of our experiences of God.

I think there may well be found here also a clue to the subtle part which morality plays in original Buddhism. Buddhism is much more than morality, but of this 'more' little can be expressly said except in terms of its toning through moral ingredients, the Way and the Goal being peculiarly interconnected. If this view can be justified, it also shows Buddhism as having exceptional significance for our understanding of religion today.

These matters must finally be set against the background to Buddha's life. We do not know how well, if at all, he knew the *Upanisads* themselves. But he was bred in a community imbued by their spirit and the spirit which produced them; they presided over his original quest. He may have turned away from much of their teaching and the practices derived from them in his day, but his innovations may yet have much in common with what he thought he rejected. If we look for the affinities in the substance rather than the form of his more elusive claims, and bring to our task a creative religious insight of our own, then I think we shall finally come to this conclusion: firstly, that 'enlightenment' stands for Buddha for some positive state of inner peace, and, secondly, that the account which is given of the way this state is attained, the impression that Buddha himself underwent some overwhelming experience, similar, both in itself and in its accompaniments, to those of other great contemplatives, together with the impact he made on others, as reflected in legend as well as in devotion to him – that all these considerations seem to combine with Buddha's silence and negativism as mutually supporting strands of cumulative evidence showing that the silence was in fact the caution of one who sensed how difficult, and even dangerous, it was to characterize directly the supreme religious reality. Do we not in fact find this in the *Upanisads* also, even to the extent of learning of some teachers who expressly enjoined silence as the answer to religious questions? Whether that silence can also be broken, and what in that case must be our final verdict on Buddhism, are other matters that cannot be considered at the moment.

I conclude therefore that the more we appreciate, as we seem to do today in the many very different lines of thought that converge on religion, ranging from transcendental theology to positivism, that express characterization of the ultimate nature of God is out of the question, and much more so its rationalization, the better prepared we are to see in the alleged agnosticism of Buddha the sort of atheism which is sometimes described as an essential element of faith; and I think we can understand this more plainly when it is seen as a continuous feature in a religious tradition of considerable antiquity in which the coming into greater explicitness of a genuine sense of the transcendent, as involved in religion at all times, is an outstanding feature.

VIII

Religion is not however concerned merely with the being of God – or of some ultimate supreme reality whether thought of as God or not. Further affirmations are made about this reality, and this at once presents us with an exceptionally difficult and central problem for all thinking about religion, namely how can any affirmation at all be made about a transcendent reality. This is not an accentuation of the difficulties we normally find in affirming certain things about elusive and mysterious realities. For the mystery in the case of the transcendent is peculiar. It is total. The difficulties we find in other spheres may well be insurmountable in practice, but we can at least hope for some clue to the solution of our problem, some guide to the nature of the mysteries to be reduced, in the sort of things we understand already. There is some community of nature and continuity in all finite reality, we explain one thing and learn about it in terms of its relation to others. But it is the ultimate inadequacy of this kind of explanation that leads us to recognize the inevitability of a transcendent reality, some ground of limited finite being which is complete and unconditioned as finite things cannot be. This is the logic of the move from the finite to the infinite, however in practice the relevant insight is induced. But by its very nature it seems to rule out predications, the affirming of one thing or another and the determination which is also negation and exclusion. God becomes in this sense altogether elusive, He is 'wholly other' or 'beyond' in the most absolute way. It seems thus impossible to know anything about Him other than that He must be as the ground of all other reality, we can affirm His being but, in a way quite unlike anything else, without any explicit apprehension of anything further which this involves. The recognition of transcendence seems to be the recognition of absolute mystery.

How then does it come about that we do claim to reduce this mystery? How is it that some religions speak in exceptionally intimate ways about God and His dealings with men? This is the problem of revelation and divine disclosure, and it must be stressed again that this is not merely the problem of indicating how in fact divine disclosure takes place but also the basic epistemological problem of how any communication of this kind is possible, since by the nature of the case there appears to be an insurmountable barrier between God and man at the point where communication could begin to be possible.

It does not help this problem in the least to convert this barrier into anything other than it really is, namely the inevitable consequence of the distinction of finite and infinite. Some have converted it into a problem of certain particular relations of God and man, and in this way they have blurred the logical and epistemological character of the problem. The barrier in question becomes, for example, the barrier of sin, a barrier in some way set up by man himself, inevitable as human nature is now perhaps, but not ultimately and inherently so; and the removal of the barrier (and the solution of problems concerning it) becomes in this way a matter of modes of dealing with a sinful state or with the blindness of those who hold down the truth in unrighteousness. This becomes more plausible because sin does undoubtedly affect profoundly the way divine disclosure becomes in fact possible, and the state to which it is addressed. But this is a problem in itself, a further complication, and we ought not to be induced to forget the initial epistemological problem by diverting attention to any further complications that attend the relationship of God and man as we find them in practice. The barrier of finite and infinite is not initially the barrier of sin, it functions directly on its own account.

It is for this reason very unfortunate that those who have had the profoundest sense of God's transcendence in recent times, and who have on this basis recalled us from an easy rationalist liberalism to a true sense of the depth and mysteriousness of religious reality, have belied and distorted their own profoundest insight by a most improper conflation of logical and ethical considerations. They have been helped to do this by their supposition that it confirmed them in their hold on a form of traditional doctrine which makes all men the inevitable victims of an original transgression in which also they mysteriously have a part. The difficulties of this doctrine are themselves welcomed, under the more dignified name of paradox, as an indication of essential mystery at the core of religion – the more perplexing the doctrine the better, the more is it indicative of the elusive transcendent reality with which we deal. But this is sheer confusion and it can but lead to an exceedingly mischievous glorification of unreason. The mystery of religion is *sui generis* and there is no proper indication of it in avoidable paradoxes and contradictions in our thought in other regards. The essential mystery of religion may invest every aspect of reality as it affects it, but the way this comes about can only be properly understood if we have a proper appreciation at the outset of the way the mystery initially and essentially presents itself. It arises, as I said, directly from the contrast of finite and infinite.

This problem is not, however, quite as acute for some religions as for others. There are religions which do not make the bold affirmations about God which are so crucial for Christianity. They are able to do this because they have not the same concern about our status as finite creatures. Indeed they do not think of us as distinct created beings at all. Fortitude is not ultimate. It is at best a phase of our being to be superseded in the end; and, in most versions of this kind of monistic religion, the finite is ultimately an illusion, some way in which things appear at present but not the proper truth about them. The only ultimately real is the Supreme Self, the One Mind in all minds; and the problem therefore is not that of attaining, *qua* finite being, some saving apprehension of infinite Being. It is rather a matter of passing beyond the state or sphere where such a question can arise, of becoming wholly identified with the one ultimate reality or of realizing that we are in fact identified with it always. The problem of the here and now is not insistent, or if it is it can only be in the form of seeking most effectively to transcend the here and now. Disciplines, devotions, techniques of meditation, the day-to-day round of religious observances, all centre on this one aim of 'passing beyond', not just beyond our present temporal state, but beyond temporality and finitude as such. Salvation is in this way by transcendence of self out of all particularity, and so the problem of particularity and of limited finite existence, including the crucial religious question of how the finite, in its unmitigated finitude, can have any relation, cognitive or any other, with the infinite, is passed by and does not become obtrusive where the emphasis is upon drawing away from finite existence altogether.

This does not mean that we never have particular affirmations in religions like Hinduism or Buddhism. We have plenty of a sort, but they have nothing of the firmness or finality of Christian claims. They are aids or stages on the way, substitutes for them are found, their adequacy is partial and suited to our particular need and understanding at the time, and in due course we shall pass beyond them and cast them aside as childish things in our attainment of our ultimate vision of the one reality in which all else is contained, indeed not a vision any more but the transcendence of all determination and apprehension of the kind which is only too familiar to us now. Problems of adequacy there will be in some measure, but the concern with them is more pragmatic than final; and there is certainly no once for all redeeming event whose significance is to be preserved at all cost, nothing is just once for all and nothing has cosmic significance other than the superseding of all signification in the normal sense.

This difference is well reflected in the radically different accounts which Buddha and Jesus took of their own roles. When Buddha, at the time of his death, was asked how it would be best to remember him he simply urged his followers not to trouble themselves about such a question. It did not matter much whether they remembered him or not, the essential thing was the teaching – and what mattered about the teaching was the *Way*, to live so that at last, in this life or later, illumination and release would be ours too. It is almost, in this regard, like a scientific doctrine; it does not matter all that who propounded it provided we can understand and use it now. Its importance is in no way bound up with the way it was discovered. We can understand it without knowing anything of its inventor. But this is not the way of Christian truth. This is somehow given in event and is historical in essentials; and so it is that we find that Jesus, the embodiment of self-denial and humility, also puts Himself at the centre of redeeming activity. He is Himself the way, the truth and the life, and his disciples, far from forgetting who He was or what He did Himself, are to come to Him, to be drawn to Him and in sacramental worship to 'do this in remembrance of Me'.

There have not been lacking however voices of protest, within Hinduism especially, against the excessive depreciation of the particular and the here and now. This does not take the form of ascribing decisive importance to special historical events, as in Christianity. But there have been rigorous pleas for a firmer recognition of the events of the present life as having importance on their own account and not to be entirely absorbed in the One Ultimate or Absolute Being. Such pleas have even been presented on occasion in the language of Christianity, but the import of them has never been wholly Christian, nor has the veneration of Jesus acclaimed Him as the one final mediator between God and man. The Christian terms are used in a less exclusive sense than in orthodox Christianity. Even so, there is a very significant move towards the recognition of the historical as having importance on its own account and an indispensable role in religion.

IX

Perhaps no one represents this emphasis within the Hindu religion itself so well as the recent thinker and reformer Sri Aurobindo. Born in 1872 and completing his formal education with a distinguished record in Classics at Cambridge he returned to India to become a leading thinker and reformer whose philosophical work should be of exceptional interest today to those who are concerned to find instructive meeting points of East and West. He pleaded vigorously for the place of philosophy in religion. 'Without philosophy', he declared, 'religion degenerates into superstition and obscurantism, philosophy without religion is barren.' Not all would subscribe to the latter half of this declaration, but it should be remembered that Aurobindo was thinking here primarily of metaphysics in the broadest sense, and in that context there is more to be said for his view. It seems to me certainly true that, in the growing sophistication of our times religion that dispenses with philosophy is apt to degenerate into superstition, more or less refined according to its votaries. In one way or another there has always been a philosophical aspect to Hinduism and this is a feature of religion which a perceptive Hindu thinker can effectively bring to the notice of the western world at a time when many religious people, including philosophers, are disposed to resent the intrusion of philosophy on the domain of religion.

By way of correcting the prevailing tendency in Hindu religion Aurobindo insists that his own religion of Hinduism ought to become more dynamic, there should be felt within it more of what is sometimes described today by western theologians as the 'power of being', a sense of the transcendent at work within present reality, elevating and transforming it and making its own reality known in the difference it makes in the here and now. This is not to reduce religion to humanism, as so often happens today in the West where there is felt a deep concern for the contemporary relevance of religion. Orientalists have a shrewd lesson to teach us here. They are more adept in some ways at avoiding extremes. This is the bright side of a medal which has on the dimmer side a tendency towards too easy a conflation or syncretism of opposing views. Not to generalize too much, Aurobindo has certainly pointed out well the way to understand the Beyond, as a genuinely different dimension of being, in the way it manifests itself in the world of finite experience. Pantheism in its various forms is firmly avoided, God is not just a totality of things and He is not strictly identified with present reality, but He is known in a dynamic quality His presence in the world lends to the events of the present life. This is the main significance of Aurobindo's teaching about the 'Life Divine'.

A more specific feature of this emphasis on the world beyond making itself felt within the present world is the insistence on the interiority of all experience. There is nothing occult or ecstatic about this. It is just the recognition that all spiritual activity is in a sense a 'life within' which is reflected in outward behaviour and attitudes. This contrasts sharply with the fashion that prevails in contemporary western philosophy where, in many influential quarters, the repudiation of any finite access to our own thoughts and experiences is almost axiomatic. Variations on the verification principle and on linguistic offshoots of it which only thinly disguise the original and continuing motif, have involved for many the *a priori* refusal to acknowledge any reality that is not observable and in principle capable of being known exhaustively in the terms in which the external world is known. Subtle variations on these behaviouristic accounts of experience abound, and this is not the place to comment further upon them or seek to refute them. But those who are concerned to re-establish the inwardness or privacy of experience as it is for the individual without lapsing into a misleading postulation of pseudo entities can benefit much from careful heed to the subtle way the interiority of experience is handled by Aurobindo. He appreciates well how exposed his position would be if the alleged inner life of the spirit were to be modelled too closely on the way we refer to external reality, and the temptation to fall into the latter error besets him less than his western counterparts whose concepts are apt to be unduly influenced by the more materialistic and practical bent of our recent culture.

There are in Aurobindo's writings, moreover, striking indications of the way the interiority of our own experience affords a clue to the way we are able to make significant reference to the even more elusive reality of the transcendent. This is not a new approach to religious questions, but not many have grasped its true importance or appreciated properly how it operates. In times past Augustine, among Christian thinkers, had a very fine discernment of the true nature of the analogy of our knowledge of one another's hidden inner life with our knowledge of God, although this is a feature of Augustine's teaching which has been much obscured by the unfortunate representation of his thought for many exclusively in terms of what has since come to be known as Augustinian doctrines of sin and the Fall. The latter gives us only one side of Augustine's thought, and not in my view the most helpful and illuminating. On its other side it is peculiarly relevant to the consideration of the epistemological problems of religion in the shape they have today, and what is suggestive in the line we can trace from Augustine through Descartes to Tennant and James Ward today has, in the handling of similar themes by Aurobindo, an analogue that is sufficiently like to be relevant and unlike enough to be suggestive and to open up fresh possibilities. A comparison of these two thinkers in the present regard, coming as they do from such very different periods and different religious contexts and cultures, could be very illuminating at the present day.

Nor is it surprising, in the light of these features of Aurobindo's thought, that he should also have concerned himself much with paranormal phenomena and their significance for religion. Here again his attitude is temperate and judicious. He stresses the need to have the right conceptual framework for the investigation and further handling of such phenomena, a need which has sometimes been overlooked, to the detriment of experiment, by some western investigators. He has a confident expectation of an extension of paranormal powers to include the more controlled exercise of them and their manifestation in more normal contexts of waking experience and less in states of sleep or trance. At the same time he has a shrewd appreciation of the limitation of this approach to the problems of religion. In essentials, he tells, it offers no more than 'a larger field of phenomena'.[1] The radical questions remain the same; and in this Aurobindo, in spite of his considerable confidence in the extension of paranormal powers, shows himself wiser than many who interest themselves in the same phenomena in the West. He holds the subject in a very clear perspective. This is also true of his account of the problem of revelation and the authority of scriptures. To anyone who is deeply concerned about our recognition of a Power from beyond the world which is all the same active within the world and known to us in that way, the problem of recognizing what is divine in present experience leads easily to the problem of what is alleged to have been disclosed in various ways in times past. Hinduism, like other religions, has a very substantial body of sacred literature, and the recognition of the authority of

1. *The Life Divine*, p. 77.

this literature is an important feature of Hinduism. But this literature is of a highly varied kind and it is not bound up, in the same way as the Christian Bible, with a distinct historical tradition and prophetic figures standing in a fairly firm relation to one another and to certain central historical events. The problem of the authority of scriptures is thus a considerable problem for Hindu thought, but not in precisely the same way as in the Christian tradition. Aurobindo has concerned himself much with this problem. He is not of course the first to do so, the problem has been central to Hindu thought and scholarship for a long time. But Aurobindo has brought to it the freshness of a mind steeped in western thought and standards of scholarship and he has said some extremely penetrating things, in this context, about religious imagery and symbolism. He anticipates much that recent western scholars have said about 'the life of images'. It is not easy to quote the most effective passages out of their contexts. But the following observations will at least give an indication of the good sense which Aurobindo brings to the treatment of these questions:

Religious forms and systems become effete and corrupt and have to be destroyed, or they lose much of their inner sense and become clouded in knowledge and injurious in practice, and in destroying what is effete or in negating aberrations reason has played an important part in religious history. But in its endeavour to get rid of the superstition and ignorance which have attached themselves to religious forms and symbols, intellectual reason unenlightened by spiritual knowledge tends to deny and, so far as it can, to destroy the truth and the experience which was contained in them.[1]

But the point of greatest importance for us comes in the rigour of Aurobindo's protests against the other-worldly character of much traditional Hinduism and the general

1. *The Human Cycle*, p. 177.

effect of the attitude of mind so engendered. His denunciations of what he finds amiss in his own religion are not peculiar to him, and they may be too sweeping and unqualified. But I think they are of considerable interest as indications of the attitude of a recent Hindu thinker towards the aspect of Hinduism which the West has usually found most disconcerting. That the criticism comes from within the religion itself and from the pen of a person who has spent himself in the devoted service of his own culture and religion lends it peculiar weight. I shall quote at some length and leave the passages reproduced to indicate in their own way a significant meeting point of East and West in contemporary thought.

Aurobindo writes:

Individual salvation can have no real sense if existence in the cosmos is itself an illusion. In the monistic view the individual soul is one with the Supreme, its sense of separateness an ignorance, escape from the sense of separateness and identity with the Supreme its salvation. But who then profits by this escape? Not the supreme Self, for it is supposed to be always and inalienably free, still, silent, pure. Not the world, for that remains constantly in the bondage and is not freed by the escape of any individual soul from the universal illusion. It is the individual soul itself which effects its supreme good by escaping from the sorrow and the division into the peace and the bliss. There would seem then to be some kind of reality of the individual soul as distinct from the world and from the Supreme even in the event of freedom and illumination. But for the illusionist the individual soul is an illusion and nonexistent except in the inexplicable mystery of *māyā*. Therefore we arrive at the escape of an illusory non-existent soul from an illusory non-existent bondage in an illusory non-existent world as the supreme good which that non-existent soul has to pursue! For this is the last word of the knowledge, 'There is none bound, none freed, none seeking to be free.' *Vidyā* turns out to be as much a part of the Phenomenal as *avidyā*, *māyā* meets us even in our escape and laughs at the triumphant logic which seemed to cut the knot of her mystery.[1]

He continues:

The principle of negation prevails over the principle of affirmation and becomes universal and absolute. Thence arise the great world-negating religions and philosophies; thence too a recoil of the life motive from itself and a seeking after a life elsewhere flawless and eternal or a will to annul life itself in an immobile reality or an original non-existence. In India the philosophy of world-negation has been given formulations of supreme power and value by two of the greatest of her thinkers, Buddha and Shankara. There have been intermediate or later in time, other philosophies of considerable importance, some of them widely accepted, formulated with much acumen of thought by men of genius and spiritual insight, which disputed with more or less force and success the conclusions of these two great metaphysical systems, but none has been put forward with an equal force of presentation or drive of personality or had a similar massive effect. The spirit of these two remarkable spiritual philosophies – for Shankara in the historical process of India's philosophical mind takes up, completes and replaces Buddha – has weighed with a tremendous power on her thought, religion and general mentality: everywhere broods its mighty shadow, everywhere is the impress of the three great formulas, the chain of *karma*, escape from the wheel of rebirth, *māyā*.[2]

He writes in the same vein about traditional Indian thought as he understands it:

Human, social and political endeavour turns always in a circle and leads nowhere; man's life and nature remain always the same, always imperfect, and neither laws nor institutions nor education nor philosophy nor morality nor religious teachings have succeeded in producing the perfect man, still less a perfect humanity – straighten the tail of the dog as you

1. *The Life Divine*, p. 47.   2. op. cit., p. 493.

will, it has been said, it always resumes its natural curve of crookedness. Altruism, philanthropy and service, Christian love or Buddhist compassion have not made the world a whit happier, they only give infinitesimal bits of momentary relief here and there, throw drops on the fire of the world's suffering. All aims are in the end transitory and futile, all achievements unsatisfying or evanescent; all works are so much labour of effort and success and failure which consummate nothing definitive: whatever changes are made in human life are of the form only and these forms pursue each other in a futile circle; for the essence of life, its general character remains the same for ever. This view of things may be exaggerated, but it has an undeniable force; it is supported by the experience of man's centuries and it carries in itself a significance which at one time or another comes upon the mind with an overwhelming air of self-evidence.[1]

Yet again he writes:

But in the theory of illusion the only reality is an indeterminable featureless pure Existence, Brahman, and there is no possibility of its being translated or mistranslated into a system of symbol-figures, for that could only be if this Existence had some determinate contents or some unmanifested truths of its being which could be transcribed into the forms or names given to them by our consciousness: a pure indeterminable cannot be rendered by a transcript, a multitude of representative differentiae, a crowd of symbols or images; for there is in it only a pure identity, there is nothing to transcribe, nothing to symbolize, nothing to image. Therefore the dream analogy fails us altogether and is better put out of the way; it can always be used as a vivid metaphor of a certain attitude our mind can take towards its experiences, but it has no value for a metaphysical enquiry into the reality and fundamental significances or the origin of existence.[2]

In terms such as these then, and in language almost intemperate at times, Aurobindo voices his protest and

1. op. cit., p. 495.   2. op. cit., p. 509.

seeks to bring his religion into closer accord with the here and now which is also the focus of attention among leaders of thought in western religions at present. Here a reformed Hinduism comes very near to Christianity, and it can often, as in the case of Aurobindo himself, make extensive use of Christian language and come very close to Christianity in practice and spirit. It does this in a healthy way as, in Aurobindo's thought, the emphasis on the here and now contains no suggestion of reducing the Beyond to its manifestations in the present. That is a temptation to which many Christian apologists have succumbed. They have presented the substance of religion in terms of moral endeavour or some peculiar slant we may have on our present existence or some alleged depth of our own being. They have been driven to this in two ways, firstly through philosophical difficulties about the reality of any existence not directly verifiable in present experience and secondly (and more pragmatically), by the difficulty of making the traditional language of religion and the action of an eternal transcendent reality meaningful at all to our contemporaries. Indication of this attitude and the consequent short way with the unbeliever, the radical attenuation of faith, has already been given. I myself consider this form of apologetic ambiguity or capitulation most regrettable, and for that reason I find it also refreshing to examine the work of a recent Indian thinker who lacks none of the contemporary sense of the present and the need to be religiously articulate in the here and now, but who interprets this firmly in terms of making a reality which is altogether beyond finite life of distinctive account for us in the substance of finite experience. The beyond is allowed to be elusive, and the problem of religious language and symbolism is thus known to be uniquely difficult, but it is all the same clearly understood as a problem with the twin terms of the finite and the infinite. This offers no short way with the task of giving religion a truly contemporary relevance.

X

But however close Hinduism may come in these ways to enlightened forms of Christianity today, there remain radical differences which cannot be surmounted without surrender of essential features of these religions. These differences turn on the 'once for all' character of the distinctively Christian means of grace and salvation, involving as these do unique and unrepeatable redeeming activity. This is the essential stumbling block and the main reason for the impossibility of integrating the Christian religion with other faiths. The idea of incarnation itself is of course anathema to a religion like Islam which has otherwise much in common with Christianity. The Muslim understands the notion of God's transcendence and absolute majesty in a way which altogether precludes His becoming less than absolute being or having the form of a man. Any notion of incarnation is at once for the Muslim idolatrous, and Islam has set itself with great fierceness against any worship of idols. This is in line with the most express teaching of Muhammad, in spite of the curious wavering of the Prophet himself on one critical occasion. Muslims who have deviated from the tradition in this respect have been regarded as peculiarly objectionable heretics. But Hinduism has never had much reluctance to thinking in terms of divine incarnations. Indeed the belief in the recurring avatar, of God coming down in human form as need arises is a very prominent feature of Hinduism. But this is none the less a very different notion of incarnation to the one we find in Christianity – and a much more restricted one. The difference may not be easy to indicate, indeed it is an exceptionally difficult task to do so

197

properly, but this is the point above all on which true understanding of Christianity turns.

The last point needs to be emphasized especially in a Christian context. The Christian religion, today as in the past, stands or falls with it, and many who are concerned with the commendation and defence of Christianity today have grievously misjudged their task, and underestimated its difficulty, when they have sought to ease the way for themselves by various mitigations of the uniqueness and distinctness of the Christian notion of Incarnation. There have, admittedly, been very crude versions of the essential Christian claims; and it is a good service to Christianity to expose and criticize these. But, from the Christian point of view, the criticism should proceed on the basis of a more profound understanding of the truth which is travestied in crude incarnational doctrines. The essential task of Christian apologetics centres on the acquisition of a deep insight into the meaning to be given to the idea of incarnation in a Christian context and the ways of making this significant at present.

The difference between Christianity, in the present regard, and other religions is much affected by radical differences of opinion on the status of finite beings, and the clue to the basic difference here is found in the idea of creation. In the Hebrew-Christian tradition we have a profound understanding of the way the transcendence of God requires all other being to be distinct from Him. Finite reality depends on God but is never merged in the reality of God, and with this there went also a sharp appreciation, much intensified in Christian understanding, of the ultimacy and finality of personal existence.

This went along with a special awareness of the personal nature of God, not as something we can properly understand but as something we encounter in the dealings of God with us. There are of course many intimations of the personal character of God in other religions, notably in the Bhakti forms of Hinduism. But they take the form of a vague and general sense of God as personal being, and it is questionable how ultimate this is, since it rarely, if ever, overrides the general Hindu affirmation of *karma* and its inexorable operation. The theism we find within Indian religions is certainly not derived from a sense of sustained and patterned intervention in history, it has its source more in occasional unorganized experience in which a formative influence from without is generally sensed as personal encounter. In the Christian religion the intensified sense of the distinctness and ultimacy of persons carries with it a sense of the personal character of God being intimately and firmly known in the dealings of an essentially transcendent Being with men in the substance of sustained and developing personal experience.

This means also that there is a restricted qualified character to the notion of incarnation in Hinduism. As an Indian writer has recently put it: 'An *avatar* may enter human life, but he does not share it. He is over and above it, always God, helping, guiding, instructing, but as God'.[1] There is no real identification with finite existence. In the Christian notion of the Incarnation however God becomes 'truly man', and the main formative task of early Christian theology was to establish this claim against attractive alternatives which made the faith easier in some ways to understand and accept. In the essential Christian claim there is no compromise over either the complete divinity or the complete humanity of Jesus.

But this is not just a matter for bold affirmation or blind appeal to authority. It must be understood, even though that in itself implies that there is much in the Christian claim which cannot be properly understood. That the same being is strictly both God and man is an astounding claim and no

1. Sabaputhy Kulandran, *Grace in Christianity and Hinduism*, p. 264.

one should commend the Christian faith without a deep and daunting sense of the heroic dimensions of the claim he makes. It is not a limited claim to be apprehended in the context of a universe where the distinction of finite and infinite is not ultimate, where the divine is in some way all-pervasive and the finite has some elements of divinity within it, if only as appearance. 'Very God, very man', are notions which have both to be taken in the strictest sense by the Christian. But for this very reason it is all the more important to indicate clearly how this astonishing, and initially preposterous affirmation – blasphemous to Jews or Muslims and folly to the Greeks – comes to be made, and this is where philosophy has a uniquely important part to play in the understanding of the Christian religion today and in setting out the differences between it and other religions even where they may seem superficially similar. This makes it extremely regrettable, to the point one might almost say of tragedy, that philosophy in the service of religion has been so extensively repudiated, not least in the quarters where there is the most inspired prophetic understanding of the nature of religion and its place in the world as we find it today.

A hint has already been given of how alien the distinctively Christian ideas seem to most people today, most of all in the western parts of the world where the Christian faith has prevailed in the past. 'Incarnation', 'atonement', 'redemption', 'grace', 'salvation', 'reconciliation', to say nothing of vivid metaphors like 'being washed in the blood of the Lamb', are words which convey hardly any meaning to the younger generations of today. There are many reasons for this, the basic one being the radical change in the material conditions of existence which we have undergone. There has been more change of this kind within a few years of living memory than in many centuries of times past and perhaps a more drastic upheaval in this way than at any other period of history. Whole peoples have been torn from their cultural roots, and ideas which depend on the perpetuation of a live tradition are, in this situation, apt to be devoid of all significance. The task of Christian apologetics is to make these traditional notions significant in the life of today. Some try to do this by sheer emphatic assertion, others by using the traditional terms for attenuated ideas easy of acceptance in terms of prevailing beliefs of today. Neither of these short cuts will meet the situation. We need to rediscover the essential original meaning of central Christian affirmations and without philosophy the prospect for doing so is bleak indeed.

XI

On one side the task of philosophy here concerns the effective exhibition of that elusive mystery and transcendence of God noted already. This will bring out points of affinity and difference between religions, in respect of their understanding of the Being of God, in the way already indicated. It will help also to show the peculiarity of the Hebrew-Christian understanding of God's transcendence as itself involving the distinctness of other reality and, consequent on that, there can be exhibited those patterns of divine intervention in human experience through which the particular and personal character of God, in His relation to us, can be known. But to exhibit this effectively we have to proceed to the other main side of the task of philosophy in religion, namely the presentation of a true understanding of the nature of man and his needs. The central issue here is that of the soul in relation to its body and the 'interiority' commonly ascribed to the soul but extensively questioned today. As I understand this matter, the mind is altogether distinct from the body, although of course related to it in a peculiarly intimate way – 'closely inter-mixed', as Descartes, the famous advocate of dualism of mind and body, put it. In terms of this view it is also affirmed that we know ourselves in a peculiarly intimate way by being ourselves, I know my own thoughts and sensations in having them, but I know the minds of other persons in some indirect way, usually, if not invariably, involving their bodies. These contentions have been very widely repudiated in recent philosophy, but they have also been very ably and vigorously defended, and I think the defence has been extremely successful. The issue cannot be examined afresh here, I can only refer the reader to the course of recent controversy about it, but I am myself convinced that the sort of dualism of mind and body indicated above is sound in essentials and indispensable for a Christian view. It is necessary for any belief in our survival of the dissolution of our bodies, and thus in the possibility of immortality. But it is equally necessary for a true grasp of the sort of work of reconciliation which we find described in the Christian Scriptures. It is the last point that concerns us most now.

If the mind is shown to be clearly distinct from the body the way is open for the affirmation of genuine freedom of will and responsibility. There are, of course, further ingredients in the concept of responsibility, but this is not the place to review them closely. Suffice it to affirm that in acknowledging the independent reality of mental processes we make possible the affirmation of ultimate accountability, and with this the finality of the guilt we incur for wrongful action. This is itself an aspect of experience which has much greater prominence in western than in eastern thought, but it concerns us especially now in its relevance to the distinctly Christian notion of salvation, and our clue to a sound understanding of that subject today is to be sought in the ultimacy and inwardness or privacy of the individual soul.

It is not, of course, contended by any sensible person that we have awareness of no reality other than ourselves. That sort of solipsism would make nonsense of all experience. It is because Cartesian dualism has been thought to involve an extreme form of solipsism that it has been so much lampooned of late. Professor Gilbert Ryle, for example, declares that, on a Cartesian view, 'absolute solitude' is the ineluctable destiny of the soul. This is however the gravest travesty; for those who affirm that the individual knows his own thoughts and other mental processes directly or 'from within' in having them are in no way precluded from insisting that we have very full and reliable knowledge of other persons in other ways, mainly at least through observation of their bodies, noting their movements and the sounds they utter and so on. All that is claimed is that each person lives through or 'enjoys' his own experience and is in this way a world to himself. This interiority is never broken, even in the most intimate relationships. There is never a strict confluence of selves, no one strictly enters the mind of another; and this feature of the human situation has importance for religion in a great many ways. It can be argued, for example, that many perversions and distortions of human aspirations, those which culminate in the sadism and sensual perversions much publicized today, owe much of their strength to desperate and misguided attempts to break through all barriers and know other persons as they are for themselves and for God. We rebel in those ways against the inevitable consequences of our finitude, and for this the only ultimate solution is a sound understanding of our created dependent nature in its relation to the infinite Being in fellowship with whom we have our true fulfilment. We are not meant to be God or to become in any way divine, but we have every solace in knowing the love of God for us and our abiding destiny in our abiding relation to Him. This is a subject of considerable importance and vastness in itself, and I can only repeat here in very brief terms what I have outlined more fully elsewhere. But this is not the point where due appreciation of the interiority of personal experience bears most closely of all on our differing conceptions of salvation.

The crucial point concerns the effect of wrongful action and the sense of guilt which this involves on human personality. For the ultimate consequence of sin is separation, and while there can be many other forms of separation and loneliness, some of it due to the incidents of particular distressing situations, nothing is so forlorn or final, so far as human solace is concerned, as the imprisonment of the individual by himself in his own inner reality which is the effect of deliberate wickedness. Relationship with others cannot be healthily maintained along with the sense of betrayal and insincerity which wrongful action involves. The outward show and ritual of fellowship may be maintained up to a point in such conditions, but the reality of it is drained away.

This is a situation in which we are all involved in some measure. We may not always be aware of it, but men of prophetic insight and writers of fiction help us to appreciate it, and it is a very distinct feature of recent and contemporary literature that it is so preoccupied with a sense of desolation and futility as the true inner story of circumstances that appear normal and healthy to the outward view. The situation is moreover much intensified by the fact that each individual is caught up in the debilitating effect, not only of his own wrong-doing, but of the accumulation of wrong in the past. The abiding effect of sin is social and cumulative and we are the heirs of a situation where natural trust and understanding have been extensively poisoned and marred by the insidious influence of wrongful action over the ages recoiling on the agents of it in the way of an imprisonment in their own inner life which makes relationship with others uncertain and faltering. This is experienced in different measure by different people, but it is significant how much the psychological and imaginative insights of our own day disclose to us the pervasive sense of inner aimlessness and wretchedness, a sense of some kind of alarming unreality in circumstances that are formally and materially real enough, as a general characteristic of human existence. This aspect of contemporary culture is of course in part a reflection of conditions incidental to our own times of grave disillusion and confusion. But these very conditions, in inducing a more sober and realistic appraisal of our situation than the easy optimisms of an earlier day, have also predisposed us to a profounder appraisal of the general lot of men in the world.

These are matters which are gravely travestied and misunderstood in traditional Christian doctrines, most of all in those doctrines which speak of inevitable sin and collective guilt calling for a retribution met by extreme vicarious punishment. I have tilted enough elsewhere against these notions and tried to indicate how their inherent moral repugnance is matched by ill-effects in practice. But it does not follow that we are not to speak of sin or of the devastating effect of sin on our relations with one another extensively deprived as they are of the sustaining and health-giving sense of the presence of God. It was not in vain that it was said that the wages of sin is death, and it is the cold and numbing approach of this death of the spirit, which ends in the dissolution of personality, that is being widely sensed today by imaginative writers and men of keen prophetic discernment.

It is for this situation that the Christian offers a sovereign remedy. It consists in the coming of God himself to the very heart of this situation, to endure the extreme agony of it in a fully human life. The Christian must not compromise on the humanity of Jesus any more than on His divinity. Jesus lived and died in all ways as a man, God was in Him made flesh and touched by our infirmities and He endured in this way the bitter inner agony of being utterly forsaken in the moment of the breaking of His body in the face alike of fierce hostility and of ruthless unconcern. Whatever mystery and difficulty this involves, it must certainly not be assessed in purely formal terms, but on the basis of what we understand of personal relations and the way they are marred in the unmistakable course of genuine present experience. Personal experience is our main clue to the Christian doctrines of atonement and reconciliation. How this operates in detail, how God in coming in this fully human way to terms with our infirmities opens up a way of our apprehending anew, and coming afresh within the reach of, His unlimited concern, these are not matters to be further expounded here. Nor is it to the purpose to consider closely, as I have attempted to do elsewhere, the reasons we have for believing that Jesus was Himself very God bringing His work of reconciliation to completion. It must suffice to insist that here again we do not believe or affirm blindly but on evidence of peculiar divine intervention which we can much better apprehend and receive to-day when the nature of it is exhibited to us by careful philosophical analysis.

But if all this is sound it presents us also with a distinctive course of divine intervention culminating in events which have a 'once for all' nature. Salvation is universally available, however little we know of God's ways of making it available to those who do not come within the effective Christian witness to it in this life. But it is made available through a divine intervention which is inherently wholly sufficient and thus once for all. This is, at any rate, the essential Christian claim. God did not 'come down' in Jesus to meet a particular crisis in a way that might be repeated as need arose again. Nor did He merely appear, He came in complete human form to meet a universal need in a way that is adequate for all times and places and is without parallel or substitute.

XII

This is where I think contemporary Christian apologists fall into such grievous error. For in seeking, in appallingly short-sighted ways, to come to terms with prevailing fashions of thought, they have shown themselves willing, even anxious, to dispense with the element of particularity in distinctively Christian claims. Subjecting the faith to a vague attenuation, in the hope of making it easily acceptable to agnostics and atheists, baptizing much of it to undiluted humanist terms, they have also, in many instances, treated the alleged particularity of Christian affirmations as provisional and of limited significance. The supreme example of this is Paul Tillich, who, not content with extreme evasiveness and obscurity in the course of being all things to all men, unbelievers included, has latterly shown himself equally anxious to be all things to all religions. In an extremely tenuous and obscure work, *Christianity and the Encounter of the World Religions*, he brings us to this conclusion:[1]

Religion cannot come to an end, and a particular religion will be lasting to the degree in which it negates itself as a religion. Thus Christianity will be a bearer of the religious answer as long as it breaks through its own particularity.

The way to achieve this is not to relinquish one's religious tradition for the sake of a universal concept which would be nothing but a concept. The way is to penetrate into the depth of one's own religion, in devotion, thought and action. In the depth of every living religion there is a point at which the religion itself loses its importance, and that to which it points

1. pp. 96–7.

breaks through its particularity, elevating it to spiritual freedom and with it to a vision of the spiritual presence in other
expressions of the ultimate meaning of man's existence.

This is what Christianity must see in the present encounter
of the world religions.

This is extremely wide of the mark. We do not begin to do
justice to the Christian religion if we make the particular
dispensable in the way implied in this passage. Tillich
appears to surrender what is most distinctive of Christianity. The Christian has indeed the obligation to seek the
profoundest understanding of the claims that he makes,
and he must seek all the help available to him in modern
scholarship and religious insight. He must seek to make his
own experience a profound one. But however deep his
experience and however fine his understanding of it
he does not get to a level where he does not find Christ
crucified 'once for all'. The unique events narrated in the
Gospels are the core of the Christian faith. These are not to
be taken as mere symbols of something beyond them,
whether in depths of our own experience or in the absolute
being of God. They are not just pictures, but supreme
religious reality. The Christian faith, as a distinctive faith,
cannot survive the surrender of particularity. It stands
or falls with the insistence that it was God himself, in the
form of a man, who trod this earth two thousand years ago
and died between thieves on a cross. This may not be an
acceptable view, and no one should minimize the stark
difficulty of it. But it is in fact the essential Christian belief.
If we discard it, we must make it clear that we are discarding
the central thesis of the New Testament and the main item
in the faith of Christians down the ages. For this reason I
find it very misleading, indeed nauseating, to have eminent writers and religious leaders persisting in the use of
traditional, essentially incarnational, language divorced
from the realities which give them significance and bap-

tized into an entirely new usage. It is another matter for a
Hindu or Buddhist to use Christian language in a reveren-
tial way. For the likelihood of misunderstandings is not
so great, although I myself would advocate much caution
here on the part of non-Christian writers and leaders.
They should not, I admit, be debarred from borrowing
what they can sincerely take from the Christian religion,
but they must not pass beyond the point where their own
religion bids them stop. If a Christian does surrender the
particular, in the way commended by Paul Tillich, he
should announce himself boldly a unitarian. If, as in the
case of Tillich, it is not clear that he has faith in a personal
God, he should make his home among the adherents of
other faiths. Indeed, the proper place for Tillich and many
of his followers today is in the Hindu religion. It is perfectly proper in that religion to teach that there is a point
at which every religion 'breaks through its particularity',
that all our views are partial expressions of what altogether
transcends them. But this is not a consistent course for a
Christian. He can fully allow that there is much that is
hidden from him, his own scriptures stress that, it is not for
man to find out all the ways of God – we only see 'as in a
glass darkly'. It has not yet been disclosed what we shall
be, the experience the Christian hopes to attain eventually
is boundlessly rich, and he can have little conception now
of all that it involves and the varieties of being and experience he will some day enjoy. On these matters he has also
much to learn from other faiths and practices. But at no
stage does he hope to pass beyond the point where his
experience derives its character increasingly from his
realization of what God has done for him in Christ. Nor is
there a divorce of the Jesus of history from the Christ of
faith. The crucifixion did not mean, as some maintain,
the total surrender of the Jesus of history to the Christ
of faith. It was God suffering death in the form of a man,

and this remains, for the Christian, the centre for ever of his life and hope. As the Epistle to the Colossians puts it,

For by him were all things created that are in heaven, and that are in earth, visible and invisible, whether they be thrones, or dominions, or principalities, or powers: all things were created by him, and for him. And he is before all things, and by him all things consist; and he is the head of the body, the church who is the beginning, the first-born from the dead: that in all things he might have the pre-eminence. For it pleased the Father that in him should all fulness dwell.

Christianity has in this way the Jesus of History at the centre of it. It is a position He is never to vacate. This is the radical difference between Christianity and other religions which have much in common with it. The Christian may be wrong. This book is not Christian apologetics. But it is in the interest of all that the cause of truth should be served, and it is not served by cloudy affirmations which obscure radical differences of belief. It is only when we understand just where we differ, as well as where we agree, that we can best cooperate in common interests and work for the eventual triumph of the truth. We show most respect to other religions than our own when we are prepared to indicate clearly where we fail to accept them. Nor can there be any point in talk of conversion unless we know from what and to what we are to be converted.

Bibliography

PART ONE

General

BOUQUET, A. C., *Comparative Religion*, Penguin Books, 1942.

NOSS, JOHN B., *Man's Religions*, The Macmillan Company; Collier Macmillan, 1963.

KITAGAWA, JOSEPH M., *Religions of the East*, Philadelphia, The Westminster Press, 1960.

ZAEHNER, R. C. (ed.), *The Concise Encyclopaedia of Living Faiths*, Hawthorn Books, 1959.

JAMES, E. O., *Comparative Religions: An Introductory and Historical Study*, Methuen, 1938.

SLATER, ROBERT LAWSON, *World Religions and World Community*, Columbia University Press, 1963.

Hinduism

ZAEHNER, R. C., *Hinduism*, Oxford University Press, 1962.

HIRIYANNA, M., *The Essentials of Indian Philosophy*, Allen & Unwin, 1949.

MORGAN, KENNETH W. (ed.), *The Religion of the Hindus*, Ronald Press, 1953.

The Bhagavadgita translated by S. RADHAKRISHNAN, Allen & Unwin, 1948, or translated by F. EDGERTON, Harvard University Press, 1952.

Buddhism

MORGAN, KENNETH W. (ed.), *The Path of the Buddha*, Ronald Press, 1956.

HUMPHREYS, CHRISTMAS, *Buddhism*, Penguin Books, 1951.

PRATT, J. B., *The Pilgrimage of Buddhism*, Macmillan, 1928.

THOMAS, EDWARD J., *The History of Buddhist Thought*, Routledge & Kegan Paul, 1953.

CONZE, EDWARD (ed.) and others, *Buddhist Texts through the Ages*, Oxford, Bruno Cassirer, 1954.

211

PERCHERON, MAURICE, *Buddha and Buddhism*, Longmans, 1957.

Islam

GIBB, H. A. R., *Mohammedanism*, Oxford University Press, 1949.
ANDRAE, TOR, *Mohammed: the Man and his Faith*, Scribner's Sons, 1936.
SMITH, WILFRED CANTWELL, *Islam in Modern History*, Princeton University Press, 1957.
ARBERRY, A. J., *The Koran Interpreted*, Allen & Unwin, 1955.
GUILLAUME, ALFRED, *Islam*, Penguin Books, 1956.

PART TWO

FERRÉ, FREDERICK, *Language, Logic and God,* Harpers, 1961.
LEWIS, H. D., *Teach Yourself: Philosophy of Religion*, English Universities Press, 1965.
MASCALL, E. L., *Words and Images*, Longmans, 1957.
HICK, JOHN, *The Philosophy of Religion*, Prentice-Hall, 1963.
SMITH, JOHN E., *The Philosophy of Religion*, Macmillan, 1965.
RAMSEY, I. T., *Religious Language*, S.C.M. Press, 1957.
LEWIS, H. D. (ed.), *Clarity is not Enough*, Allen & Unwin, 1963.
SMART, NINIAN, *Historical Selections in the Philosophy of Religion*, S.C.M. Press, 1962.
SMART, NINIAN, *A Dialogue of Religions*, S.C.M. Press, 1960.
PARRINDER, GEOFFREY, *Comparative Religion*, Allen & Unwin, 1962.
PARRINDER, GEOFFREY, *The Christian Debate: Light from the East*, Gollancz, 1964.
ZAEHNER, R. C., *At Sundry Times*, Faber, 1958.
RADHAKRISHNAN, *The Principal Upanishads*, Allen & Unwin, 1953.
RENOU, LOUIS, *Religions of Ancient India*, Athlone Press, 1953.
JAMES, E. O., *The Worship of the Sky God*, Athlone Press, 1963.
PARRINDER, GEOFFREY, *Upanishads, Gītā and Bible*, Faber, 1962.
CONZE, E., *Buddhism, its Essence and Development*, Oxford, Cassirer, 1957.

BIBLIOGRAPHY

MURTI, T. R. V., *The Central Philosophy of Buddhism*, Allen & Unwin, 1955.

LING, TREVOR, *Buddhism and the Mythology of Evil*, Allen & Unwin, 1962.

AUROBINDO, SRI, *The Life Divine*, Sri Aurobindo Ashram, 1960.

DONELLY, MORWENNA, *Founding the Life Divine*, Rider & Co., 1955.

MASCALL, E. L., *The Secularization of Christianity*, Longmans, 1965.

KULANDRAN, SABAPUTHY, *Grace in Christianity and Hinduism*, London, Lutterworth Press, 1964.

TILLICH, PAUL, *Christianity and the Encounter of the World Religions*, Columbia University, 1963.

BRANDON, S. G. F. (ed.), *The Saviour God*, Manchester University Press, 1963.

Index

INDEX

Religion:
  and history, 187
  and oecumenical spirit, 152
  and philosophy, 20, 26, 29, 35, 39, 187, 201
  and society, 16
  Chinese, 9
  complexity, 15
  differences in religions, 145, 151
  essence of, 14, 15
  Greek, 11
  history of, 12, 13, 24, 29
  isolation, 10
  objectivity, 16, 17, 19, 20
  oriental, 11, 27-8
  phenomenology, 16, 17, 18, 22
  primitive, 9, 15, 28, 155, 159
  relevance, 197
  resemblances in religions, 145, 151
  rites, 28
  science of, 10, 12, 14, 15, 18, 21
  study of, 23
  truth in all, 11, 14
  types, 16
  value of, 17
  varieties, 10
  western concept, 35
  world religions, 63, 207*
Revelation, 116, 120, 121, 123, 183, 191
Rig Veda, 32, 33, 42, 53, 54, 155, 156, 165
Russell, Bertrand, 142
Ryle, Gilbert, 203

Sadism, 203
Salvation, 32, 43, 45, 186, 193, 197, 200, 202, 206
Sankara, 34, 35, 44, 56, 57, 58, 163, 194
Sanskrit, 71, 82, 84, 126
Sarma, Dr, 34, 58-9
Scepticism, 13, 60, 143, 158
Science, 11-12, 16, 26
  of language, 12

of religion, 10, 12, 13
Self, 162, 163, 185
Seyyed Hossein Nasr, 126-7
Shintoism, 9
Silence, 151, 163, 173
Sin, 204, 205, 206
Siva, 36, 49, 57, 58, 152
Smart, N., 24
Smith, Cantwell, 119
Snake cult, 152
Sociology, 15, 155
Socratic technique, 172
Solipsism, 203
Soothill, W. E., 77
Sovereignty of God, 109, 113, 117, 118
Spain, 10, 100
Spencer, Sidney, 127
Spinoza, 135
Sruti, 33
Svetaketu, 54
Syed Amir Ali, 115
Symbolism, 47, 50, 151, 164, 192, 195, 196
Syncretism, 152, 189

Taoism, 9, 76, 84, 87
Tennant, 190
Theism, 37, 52, 56, 58, 59, 60
Theology, 13, 19, 22, 129, 161
Tillich, Paul, 207, 209
Tolstoi, 136
Transcendence, 110, 120, 124, 130, 149, 150, 151, 152, 156, 159, 161, 162, 163, 164, 166, 171, 178, 182, 183, 184, 185, 186, 188, 196, 197, 198, 201
Turkey, 119

Underhill, Evelyn, 164
Unity, divine, 109, 122
Unreason, 185
Upanisads, 49, 53, 55, 56, 57, 159, 160, 161, 162, 163, 164, 165, 166, 169, 172, 181, 182
Urquhart, W. S., 163

221

INDEX

MORE ABOUT PENGUINS
AND PELICANS

Penguin Book News, which appears every month, contains details of all the new books issued by Penguins as they are published. From time to time it is supplemented by *Penguins in Print,* which is a complete list of all books currently available. (There are well over three thousand of these.)

A specimen copy of *Penguin Book News* will be sent to you free on request, and you can become a subscriber for the price of the postage – 4s. for a year's issues (including the complete lists). Just write to Dept EP, Penguin Books Ltd, Harmondsworth, Middlesex, enclosing a cheque or postal order and your name will be added to the mailing list.

Another Pelican on comparative religion is described overleaf.

Note: *Penguin Book News* and *Penguins in Print* are not available in the U.S.A. or Canada

WORLD RELIGIONS: A DIALOGUE

NINIAN SMART

If religion is largely founded on faith, and faith on revelation, which of all the revelations are we to believe? Why make the Christian leap of faith, rather than the Muslim or Buddhist one?

Very different answers to such questions would be given in different parts of the world. And in this imaginative addition to the comparative study of religions Ninian Smart has adopted the form of a dialogue between a Christian, a Jew, a Muslim, a Hindu, and two Buddhists (from Ceylon and Japan) to demonstrate how the most influential creeds differ and on what they are agreed.

The result is a fresh and at times surprising insight into the religions of the world, as the protagonists exchange their fundamental beliefs about God and the Trinity, salvation, incarnation, good and evil.